Provocations

Provocations

The Story of Mrs. M

John Rouse
St. Peter's College

National Council of Teachers of English
1111 W. Kenyon Road, Urbana, Illinois 61801-1096

NCTE Editorial Board: Keith Gilyard, Ronald Jobe, Joyce Kinkead, Louise Wetherbee Phelps, Gladys Veidemanis, Charles Suhor, chair, *ex officio*, Michael Spooner, *ex officio*

Staff Editors: Sheila A. Ryan and Marlo Welshons

Cover Design: Victoria Martin Pohlmann

Interior Design: The design of this book was patterned after the design used in *Evolving Perspectives on Computers and Composition Studies: Questions for the 1990s* (NCTE and Computers and Composition Press, James R. Kalmbach, designer).

NCTE Stock Number: 37946-3050

Library of Congress Cataloging-in-Publication Data

Rouse, John, 1926–
  Provocations : the story of Mrs. M. / John Rouse.
      p.   cm.
    ISBN 0-8141-3794-6
    1. Language arts (Secondary)—United States—Case studies.
  2. English language—Study and teaching (Secondary)—United States—Case studies.   3. English teachers—United States—Case studies.
  I. Title.
  LB1631.R66   1993
  428'.0071'273—dc20   93-23398
                                                                    CIP

Contents

Preface   vii

1. Eager To Be Known   1

2. To Have the Name of Action   11

3. The Economy of Attention   23

4. When Time Is Broke   43

5. The Concealments of Style   65

6. Missing in September   89

Author   103

Preface

Somehow the activities that worked so well for Mrs. Martinez rarely worked as well for me. She had a way of getting a roomful of adolescents *going*, and I watched her at work many times, wanting to learn the secret, thinking it must lie in the ingenuity of her lessons. But those same lessons when transferred to my classroom were often received indifferently. And when I complained of this, she said "Oh, don't take me as a model. It's very complimentary but I don't think everyone can or should do the things I do." That hurt me, the thought that maybe I couldn't do it.

I said, "That hurts! You're telling me I'm condemned to be ordinary. It's like wanting to be a concert pianist, so the family brings in an old virtuoso to hear you play—you remember that story of Somerset Maugham's?—and she tells you, well you're very good but you're never going to be in the first rank. I've forgotten how the story ended. Suicide, maybe."

"You have a way of dramatizing yourself," she said. "And that can be useful. Young people like to be around someone who gets so personally involved."

"You're only trying to make me feel better—it was a disaster! I remember how they wrote those poems for you, but I try it and all they do for me is fool around. So maybe you're right, I can't do it."

"Oh, I didn't say that! But we have to work within our limitations—and that's the art of it, you know, to make something good come of them. You may not have my limitations, that's all I'm saying."

Was this her idea of encouragement? She was shifting attention away from my failure with the lesson, but now my hope for success with young people was going to depend on my limitations and that was not something I cared to think about. When we are young we like to believe we can do anything. Yet she was right, I suppose, in that art is born of limitation and depends on a particular talent working within the narrow range of one's deepest sympathies. And so the art of teaching cannot be a matter of devising one clever activity after another, but of developing a probing pattern of interest which excludes much in order to reach deeply and draw forth the telling expression.

We each will find our own way—and yet I learned from Mrs. M. She was able to develop with young people the feeling that something good was going to happen, and this expectation carried them along with her to unexpected results. Many of their days with her were of course quite ordinary, but then to break the routine she would instigate a seemingly random or spontaneous activity that was really yet another step in an ongoing way of life. It may not be a way of life for everyone who works with young people, but so that others may decide for themselves I have done my best in this book to show Mrs. M at work over her long career.

Acknowledgments

The telling of this story owes much to many conversations with Vitaly Keis, Gordon Pradl, and Ernest McClain. In Chapter 2, the second paragraph borrows several phrases from *The Social Psychology of George Herbert Mead*, edited by Anselm Strauss; and the remarks about Trickster owe something to Paul Radin's study in Native American mythology, *The Trickster*, and to the essay by Karl Kerényi included there. Also, the story Mrs. M tells about Whirlwind in this chapter has been found in *Saynday's People* by Alice Marriott, and is retold here with the permission of her estate. Chapter 4 draws on George Packer's *The Village of Waiting* and Jules Henry's *On Education*. The remark in Chapter 5 that "To be is to be perceived" is from the philosopher George Berkeley.

Chapter 1

Eager To Be Known

A teacher is one who gives not instruction but provocation, so that a learner, startled into making an assertion, begins an individual movement toward some as yet uncertain goal. Where an instructor would be concerned with the material to be covered by the class together, a teacher is concerned with the experience of individual learners. And will in fact separate learners, by whatever artful means, by cunning even, from the safe anonymity of the group in which they sit, for anonymity is an expression of the impersonal and the irresponsible. Provoked, the learner comes out of hiding long enough to express a feeling or thought which until then may have been hardly admitted or even recognized, reporting the world as beheld from one's own perspective so that a mode of being is revealed and opened to thought.

Mrs. Martinez was perhaps the most provocative person I have known, in school or out. But whether she had a natural talent for upsetting people or had developed this skill over time with practice I hardly knew at first. Her manner was not at all challenging but rather inquisitive, innocently offhand and unassuming. She would make a remark that touched a sensitive spot and so startle a person into some self-revelation or self-exposure while she listened in a most interested and sympathetic way. She could make people feel uncomfortable while giving the impression that she was the one person truly interested in their distress. They listened to her warily, expectantly.

Not that she talked very much. She was never eager to report her opinions or concerns or the events of her day, preferring rather to listen. But she wanted to make sure that something would be said worth listening to—so she would provoke people with a remark or a question, drawing out some individual response or personal story. And during the telling she was a most sympathetic and responsive listener, she charmed the soul by listening. In this way she collected many stories, she was interested in people. And sometimes she would tell a story herself, although when she was finished people often seemed uncertain how to respond because they might have sensed a concealed message in the story, an oblique reference to one's own situation or character.

"Think how you've changed since your freshman year," she told us, "how different you are. Why, by the end of this year when you graduate you will be a new person entirely—and you should all have new names, right?" We would be meeting with this woman in this classroom five times a week for the next ten months, and she seemed strange. "Now I ask you to keep this in mind so that we can find the right names for each other." She moved past her desk to the window, where she turned and looked us over again. "Will you do that?"

This must be her way of being humorous, I thought—or is this leading somewhere? My friend Gerald Robertson was sitting in front of me, and we called him Jerry. And Scott Desano, but we called him Bingo because that was a word he used a lot. And Sinful Cynthia who wasn't, except in our dreams. Finally someone said, "I already got a name."

"Yes, and you don't want to wear it out, you want to keep it fresh and full of strength. Among my people you can have several names, you can be given a new one at any turning point in your life. The first time you smile your grandmother will give you a name, because a smile means that you're becoming a person. So she gives you a name—something descriptive like Red Baby or Very Long Baby or Cry Baby. And you're called that until you are four years old, when you've changed enough to need a new name, one that fits you better, so you might be called Shining Eyes or Laughing Boy or Little Woman—something like that. Then later when you're ready to go out into the world, a secret name might be selected for you, one that will help you concentrate your powers." She hesitated. "Of course you must never tell anyone your secret name, they might use it against you. So we'll use another name for you here."

"You mean I gotta have two more names?" Jerry asked.

"Oh, you're strong enough to carry them. You look very strong to me, and the right name will make you even stronger. I know a story about that which I can tell you, and then it will be your turn to tell us something."

"Me?" Jerry said. "I got nothin to tell."

"We'll find out." She moved slowly away from the window. "What I'm going to tell you about happened a long time ago, but the story is still remembered because it reminds us of something important.

There was once a young man who lived way southwest of here in the dry country, near Sleeping Child Mesa it was, and his parents thought the time had come for him to be getting married. "There are many fine girls here," his father said. "I long for grandchildren," his mother said. And they offered to arrange a marriage for him but he refused. There was no girl around there who pleased him.

Then early one morning as he went outside he saw a fine young woman passing by the hogan alone. He spoke to her and she answered, so they went on together until the sun was almost overhead. He found her conversation as pleasing as her appearance, and as they sat together in a field of grama grass he decided to marry her.

The parents were very pleased their son had finally decided on a wife, and they welcomed her. But as the newly married ones were preparing for sleep their first night together, the young man's mother overheard a strange conversation. The new wife said, "Perhaps my people will think you have stolen me. After all, no one asked them to give me away or sent twelve horses for the bride-price. They might come to punish you. How would you escape?"

"I would call out to my father," the new husband answered, "and summon his help."

"Well," the wife said, "your father's name is Wandering Water, so perhaps he would be too long in coming. What would you do then?"

"I would call out to my mother and summon help from her clan," the husband answered.

"Well," his wife said, "your mother's name is Slower-Than-You, so perhaps she would not bring help in time. What would you do then?"

Before the young man could answer that question his mother spoke up from where she was listening. "This night is not for talking, my son," she said. And it was a good thing she did speak up because her son was about to reveal his secret name, the name that would summon the help of his guardian spirit in times of trouble.

When the coming of dawn awakened them the new wife said "Let us visit my brother and make peace between my people and yours. He will help us. After all, a husband should go with his wife's people, for that is our custom."

So in the coolness of morning they started out. But they had not gone far from the hogan when a band of men rose silently out of an arroyo, and the young man knew if they captured him he would be made a slave or killed. He called out loudly to his father but Wandering Water had already gone off. Then he called out to his mother and Slower-Than-You heard him, but by the time she reached the hogans of her people her son was already surrounded.

Then he spoke his war name under his breath and immediately felt strength flowing into his arms and swiftness into his legs. He raced through the circle of men around him, cut one with his knife as he went and ran like a deer.

A short way off he looked back, thinking of the wife left behind. His enemies had already given up the chase and only their shouts of anger could reach him. But his wife was nowhere to be seen. Near the cholla cactus where he had left her, a coyote was sitting with its head raised, watching him.

Then he knew at last that his wife was a witch, come to learn his secret name and weaken him. So he returned to the hogan alone, meeting on the way his mother's people coming to help. And so it was in that good day.

Mrs. Martinez turned and walked slowly over to the window again, where she rested an arm on the sill and leaning there looked at us, waiting. And we looked back, waiting. The silence was unusual, uncomfortable, and people began to shift uneasily in their seats, wanting to escape it, break it, but reluctant to be the first. Into the pool of stillness someone dropped a pencil, making a ripple of sound. Someone else sneezed very loudly, hoping for a laugh. And still she waited. Long silences like this were frequent with her, we learned, and even the most talkative among us would fall into a quiet reserve while feeling an increasing pressure to speak. In later years she gave up these silences, but here with us she would bide her time and wait.

"What d'ya want us to say?" someone asked.

"Whatever you like."

Again silence. Perhaps while listening to the story we had felt the qualms that make one hesitate at the beginning of an intimate relationship, with its element of the unknown, its risk. Someone said, "He left her out there and ran away."

Mrs. Martinez nodded. She stood there looking at us and we looked back at her. Finally Cynthia said, "What was that part about she wanted him to go live with her people? Was that it?"

"Oh yes! Among my people a young woman doesn't go with her husband, he goes to live with her family."

We thought about that. "Straaange," Jerry said quietly.

Mrs. Martinez nodded, waiting, but no one else spoke. What did she want? She had to be after something. The period was nearly over and we still didn't have her figured out. "Well," she said finally, "we can go back to the story later, after you've had time to think about it." She hesitated. "You know, I can see that you are serious people. And it's always possible to have a good time with people who are serious, so let's consider something else. Let's take a look at the names you've been given so far in your lives and find out what they mean."

We were agreeable, we never tired of hearing our names spoken or seeing them written in notebooks, carved on desk tops, inscribed on walls. There is always a pleasing resonance in the sound of one's own name, a satisfying elegance in its graphic representation. But of course we had no idea of the complications, the amount of work to be done over the next few days, the number of people we would be talking with about it, the dictionaries to be consulted.

There was first an original meaning of a name to uncover. Tony Esposito found out that his last name means "exposed"—referring to a baby who has been orphaned or put out to die. "In other words," Mrs. Martinez told him, "the progenitor of your clan was a foundling. You belong to the Exposed Baby Clan. Now—"

"Pooorrr baby," someone said.

"Well, yes. The name touches certain feelings in us if we know that. Up till now it's only been an abstraction, a convenient label, but there's a spirit in it. That's what we want to know about. Otherwise we might as well use numbers for you." She turned back to Tony. "Now my friend, what about your first name and your nickname? Why were you given those? And who uses them? You'll want to talk about that in your paper."

"We call'im Beetle," Jerry said.

"Oh just a moment, please! There's something you should know. Among my people we never use someone's name who is there with us and can hear it. That's considered very bad manners, like putting your hands on something that doesn't belong to you. And if you want to speak to someone you must not be chewing his name or her name in public, you find some other way to get a person's attention."

"Yeah, like 'Hey you!'" Jerry said. He sounded indignant. "We always call'im Beetle. Why d'ya want to make it so complicated?"

"So *that's* why you don't know our names," Tony said. "I mean you don't need'em, you say 'My friend.'"

"And you say things like 'This fine young lady,'" Estelle said. "I thought you were being sarcastic."

"No," Mrs. Martinez said, "I'm just trying to find the right names for you."

"I already got a name," Jerry said. "Yeah, I know—you don't wanna wear it out."

She wanted to question it. Having a name gives one a reassuring sense of personal unity, as though in hearing it we really do know who we are—but the longer we were in her classroom the more problematical that became. Everyone who knew Jerry responded differently when I said "Tell me what you think of when you hear the name Gerald Robertson." Stubborn, you can trust him, thinks he's clever, good sport, never gave me a day's worry, smartass, a real trouble-maker . . . "Hey, what d'ya mean smartass, troublemaker?" Jerry demanded. "Who you been talkin to?" For it began to seem that we have as many selves as there are people who know our names, and so would one or two or even three names be enough? Fifty minutes a day in a room with Mrs. Martinez could be a disorienting experience.

"I don't like this, what you're doing!" Jane Thomas told her, looking around to the rest of us for support. "I mean, I always liked my name but you're spoiling it."

"Well, I'm sorry about that. What's wrong?"

"You're spoiling it! I did what you told me, I looked it up, and I found out Jane means Joan. And Joan means John. It's a boy's name! And Thomas! Jane Thomas. Boys' names!"

"Well, I told you—we all need new names. Did you find out what John means?"

"Yeah, it means Grace of Jehovah, or something like that. So that's alright I guess. But the book says servants used to be called Jane. I don't like it anymore."

"Why were you given that name? Do you know?"

"From my grandmother. She's gone now, but she was this special person. Everybody called her Lady Jane. And they still talk about her."

"So people respected her, and they adjusted her name to make a better fit. She earned her name! And that's what we'll all do, right?"

"You can pick your own name," Ann said. "That's what I'm going to do. If I'm going to be a singer I can't have a name like Ann Mason—that's like a bricklayer, it's too heavy. I'm going to be Chicki Blue."

"I like it," Mrs. M told her. "And I liked hearing you sing with the glee club Friday night."

After a few discussions like this our given names were beginning to seem inadequate, arbitrary. And they're used impersonally so often as convenient labels, as a way of pointing to us that one might as well have a number as a name, like Auden's Unknown Citizen JS/07/M/378. "So take a number," Mrs. Martinez told us while we were talking about the poem. "Now—you have a nice big number, Ten Thousand, so you must feel good about that. Or would you prefer a more descriptive name?" Cynthia would but she hesitated to ask for it, knowing there already was one for her in use among the boys.

And did she really want a name that seemed to reduce her to a single aspect, like a character out of Molière or Sheridan? Yet even so, it would have some compensating values. A descriptive name, tentative and usually temporary, seems to imply that a person has possibility and will change. The giving of it may itself be a way of urging the person in some particular direction. And to meet people who have been individualized with names like Wandering Water, Slower-Than-You, Beetle, and Sinful is to feel already familiar with them, even though you may not address them by those names but must find a term for each by which to relate yourself to that individual.

Mrs. Martinez did this so easily it seemed entirely natural before long that she rarely used our names, she had an endless supply of alternatives. We learned to recognize her intention from a glance, a phrase, and her saying "my friend" seemed like a touch of her hand. But the habit came less easily to us, we kept using names. "It's easier," Jerry said. "We have to use so many words your way, so I'm just callin'im George."

"Well, let's leave him in control of his name. Now this isn't too difficult, just think a moment. What is he to you?"

"He ain't nothin to me! He's just this big guy sittin over there. Really big. I'll call'im Big Bruiser."

"No, try again. What is he to you?"

"He's a pal, okay? I'll call'im My Pal."

"That's better."

And gradually the habit caught on, so that even outside her classroom we hesitated sometimes before addressing someone by name. We made a game of finding alternatives and for a time would greet each other in the corridors or cafeteria as my esteemed classmate, the humorous one, this good sport, our well-dressed friend, and so on. In other classrooms we lived anonymously, rarely being spoken to, hardly knowing our neighbors. We listened to the teacher and answered the questions if called on, if we could, we had no reason to address anyone. But with Mrs. Martinez the ordinary rules were relaxed and there was plenty of talk, so that in her room one could become known, perhaps even understood.

Of course some people tried to take advantage of her, fooling around and making confusion. Jerry in particular, and when he was boisterous, when he reached across the aisle and pinched Cynthia, who shrieked in happy distress, Mrs. Martinez turned to him and said, "My friend, is that *our* way?" It was a question she sometimes addressed to us all, for among the Navajo a mother will say to an erring child, "That is not the Navajo way"—and she was born in Navajo country. Whatever the disturbance she never characterized our class in negative terms, she found other names for us. She liked to say that we were serious people, and in the commmunity of her classroom we felt ourselves apart from the miscellaneous others, members of a special group, of our own clan.

Yet even so there were some among us who much preferred their anonymity in other classrooms to their exposure in this, where Mrs. Martinez would pass out copies of a paper without the writer's name and after reading it aloud in her expressive voice ask, "What kind of person wrote this paper?" She would then go on to speak of the values and concerns implicit there on the page—for she specialized in the descriptive name, one that singled out some quality she wanted to encourage or turn to her purpose. Sitting with one of us and looking over a paper she might say thoughtfully, "There's something about this I don't understand. The punctuation is so sloppy—and you look like a very neat person to me." As a final comment on one paper she wrote, "This makes plain your anger here, and I can see that you are interested in people and concerned about them." She was commenting on a young man who was in fact rather self-centered but she chose to name other qualities. It seemed sometimes that one's character had become the subject of a very searching inventory. For she knew there is a power in words and people tend to become as they are named.

Jerry was sent for one day, pulled out of class and led away to the office for questioning. He denied everything—a real third degree, he told us—and finally the assistant principal said "Jerry, I know your kind and you're bad. And I will bet you right now that within six months you're going to be down in the police station." He had become an instance of a general category and so perhaps confirmed in an outlaw identity, while the individual qualities of his character went unnamed. A young person so labeled must feel a presentiment of the future that awaits, and so is tempted to take the next step toward an end that seems predestined.

But at the time Jerry only seemed more carefree than the rest of us, he enlivened the day. He thought that Mrs. M, or Mizzem as we now called her, ought to have a special name and he decided on the Hot Tamale, being careful of course to follow her practice of not saying a name within the hearing of that person. And she gave Jerry a new name early in the term because perhaps she thought he needed it then, but what it was he wouldn't tell us. That was her way, to bear young people specific witness by naming their individual qualities and so confirming them to themselves as singular and independent.

Near the end of the year, just before graduation when I thought she'd forgotten, she gave me a new name. She said, "Well, you're going out into the real world soon to fight the good fight, so you'll need a war name." And she told me mine quietly so others might not hear, and made me practice saying it till I had it right. Then she told me the meaning. Of course I must keep the name to myself to keep its power in this perilous world, for to have the right name is to have a signal in your wanderings.

Chapter 2

To Have the Name of Action

The names we have were given us by strangers who could hardly know our essential qualities—given at a first chance meeting before we even had qualities of mind or character by which to earn a name. And the infant, knowing itself at first only from the viewpoint of others, accepts its name as a natural endowment, like fingers and toes, unaware of the expectations it carries. Including very often the expectation that this new individual is to become very much like someone else. The name given to a child is the first burden it must carry in this world.

That all our actions are incomparably personal, unique, and always individual is surely true, and yet they no longer seem so when summarized under a given name, as they are in a school report. But since activity in school is carried on mainly in words, the child's developing self may gain increased definition there when youngsters are encouraged to think their own thoughts and express them in their own ways. For only after they have spoken their thoughts do they recognize themselves as the person who has said them, as this particular self who can say these particular things. So they create themselves by the gesture of the word. And their teacher comes to know them in their particularity and can name the qualities that make each youngster a unique character—introduce them to themselves, so to speak.

Of course Mrs. Martinez often thought it necessary to provoke people into action, or otherwise you would hardly get to know them. And everywhere she went she would provoke. Tranquility was a temptation to her—an empty space that needed to be filled, with argument if that's what it took to get beyond noncommittal pleasantries. As we came into the faculty room she nodded to the others already there and said "Well, what are we doing in class today?" Four bridge players were gathered around a narrow coffee table set before a battered vinyl-covered sofa. In one corner a teacher sat before a small desk marking papers. I felt adult being there for the first time, a student teacher feeling almost a professional already.

"Giving a test, of course," Hennessey said, shuffling the cards. I'd been in his math class only four years ago. "There's no point in trying to teach anything on Friday before a holiday."

"I've got book reports due," another player said. "So what're you doing?"

"I haven't decided yet." We were settling into nearby chairs, thinly upholstered. "Sometimes I like to find out what they have in mind."

"You mean you're going to make it up as you go along."

"Isn't that what we always do?"

"Some of us plan our lessons," the teacher at the desk answered.

"Well, you're very conscientious," Mrs. M said quite sincerely, as though she regretted her own shortcoming in this respect. "We should have plans." As the bridge players began their bidding she turned to me. "You saw Mark waving as we came into the building? He said something very interesting yesterday. You see, he's so scatterbrained, and I said to him awhile ago, 'Mark, sometimes I think that inside you there's a willful child,' and he laughed and said 'willful child' as though he'd never heard the expression before. Then he said, 'How old do you think the child is?' and I said, 'How old do you think?' He said, 'Thirteen, maybe—fourteen?' and I said, 'Could be.' So now he's been coming to me all year, like yesterday, and he'll say, 'I think he's about sixteen now, what do you think?'" Outside in the corridor a bell rang and we could hear the surge of youngsters passing to their next class. "I took him as my project," she said, "to see what I could do with him."

"I know that Mark and he's trouble," Hennessey said. "Sounds to me like you're trying to play psychiatrist."

"Yes, I'm trying to change him."

"But we aren't trained for that!"

"It's manipulation!" one of the card players said. "That's what you're doing, you're manipulating the kid."

"Now you've got it! That's right—I'm trying to manage that boy any way I can."

"Well, I'm not a manipulator."

"Oh go ahead and try. You'll learn to enjoy it."

As we went out to her first class I said "You got them all stirred up." By now I knew that was her way.

"Oh," she said, "they'd rather argue with me than play cards. I do a public service."

We reached her classroom and I went to sit in the back, opening my notepad as the youngsters came in. They seemed big to me, these seventeen- and eighteen-year-olds, and noisy. Soon I would have to face them myself, but for now my only task as student teacher was to observe them from the safety of my seat. Mrs. M was standing at the door greeting the youngsters as they arrived, a word for each. She did this every class period, every day. When I asked her why, she said "Because that's the only time I'll be able to speak to many of them personally, these classes are so large." Soon all thirty were in their seats and Mrs. M closed the door.

"Well," she said, "here's our last class before the holiday, and I think you have a rough day ahead of you. What should we do this period?"

"Let's have study hall," someone said. "I got a math test comin up."

"Oh no!" someone else said. "Let's do something for us." He turned to Mrs. M. "Tell us a story. You haven't told us a story in a long time." Everyone looked at her, waiting. "How about it?"

"I don't know about that," she said. "How much work have we done this week? What does our secretary say?"

Jack, currently the class secretary, flipped open a notebook. "We heard all the committee reports except from our long-haired friend over there."

"He's not ready—are you?" someone said. "Let's have the story."

"We got all our notes," Mark said, "but it's not written up yet."

"What is your report about?"

"You know what it's about. You said we spend so much time in detention we might as well write about it. So we interviewed the teacher and the principal and all the kids. Harry—I mean, my partner here—he got a lot of information. Right, Partner? He's been on detention all week. If you think we're bad news wait'll you hear about some of those guys."

"I'm looking forward to it," Mrs. Martinez said. "If I fill in for you today with a story, will your group be ready with your report the day we come back?"

"You got it!" Mark said.

"Alright—if our secretary will turn off the lights, please." She reached for the chair behind her desk and pulled it out, saying "Let's gather round." And when we had settled into a gathering, desks and chairs pulled from their regular rows, she sat there among us in the semidarkness of a cloudy morning, in the waiting silence.

"The last time we were gathered here I told you about Trickster. Do you remember the story?"

"He was like a kid," one of the boys said. "He always wanted to have everything his way."

"It was *stupid*," Lois said.

"Yes, Trickster can be very foolish. What did he do that you thought was so stupid?"

"He had a fight. I mean, his left arm had a fight with his right arm. That's pretty stupid, if you ask me."

"And what did we decide that means?"

"It's like your left hand doesn't know what your right hand is doing," someone said.

"Yeah, he just couldn't get his act together," Mark said.

"Alright. Now in this story you will see that Trickster is still just blundering along, learning everything the hard way. He still wants what he wants when he wants it and never mind anyone else. But he meets a woman who knows how to manage this kind of man, so he learns something new. It happened like this:

> Trickster was coming along in the coolness of the morn-
> ing, and as he came he saw a beautiful young woman. She
> was so beautiful he stopped right there to enjoy her beauty,

and he began to feel warm. "What a lovely woman you are," he said. "What is your name and where do you come from?"

"My name is Whirlwind," she said, "and I come from the southwest with the heat of midsummer."

"Oh that's a pretty name, Whirlwind," said Trickster. "As pretty as the rest of you. I think we ought to go along together. I will show you this fine country, and we can rest in the shade of those cottonwoods farther on."

"No," said Whirlwind, "I like to keep moving."

"Well, I'm the man who is always coming along," said Trickster, "so I'm willing to come along with you. I think maybe we ought to get married, and then we will always be together."

"Oh," said Whirlwind, "I don't want to marry you. You have funny arms and legs and a funny voice, and that funny look on your face."

"I'm very good-hearted," said Trickster. "The way I look doesn't have a thing to do with that."

"Well," said Whirlwind, "I really don't want to marry anybody. I'm too young to get married."

"Oh no you're not!" said Trickster. "You're just right for getting married. Why, anybody as beautiful as you are ought to get married right away while she's still young—before she gets old and fat and ugly, and nobody wants her."

"Well, I don't know," said Whirlwind. "My people say I'm very hard to get along with. Maybe I'd better not marry anybody."

"I'm not so easy to get along with myself," said Trickster. "Some people say I'm just mean, I'm so hard to get along with. That ought to make us a good pair."

"Of course," said Whirlwind, "when I really like somebody I'm willing to do most anything to get along with him."

"That's just the way I am," said Trickster. "Why, I'd do anything to make the person I really loved happy."

"Well," said Whirlwind, "you make us sound a lot alike."

"Oh we are," said Trickster. "I think we'd be making a big mistake not to get married. It seems to me that we were made for each other."

"Alright," said Whirlwind. "Then I guess we should get married."

Trickster was so excited that he came running to her
with his arms wide open. He wanted to catch hold of her
before she could change her mind and run away. But just
as he caught hold of her, up she went in a cloud of leaves
and grass and sticks and dust, carrying Trickster along with
her.

She carried him away, far away, and then she threw him
down on the ground near Saddle Mountain. "There!" she
said. "Maybe that will teach you a lesson. Maybe now
you'll believe what a person tells you the first time!"

And off she went, leaving him choking and sputtering
in her dust, for she really was the whirlwind.

There was a moment's silence. Mrs. M's voice coming to us
there in the semidarkness had carried us away, and we needed
time to return from Saddle Mountain to our chalkboarded room
with yellow walls. In the stories about Trickster that Mrs. M
liked to tell, we meet a being who has no purpose in life beyond
immediate gratification, no interest in others except as they may
service him—the enemy of all restraint, of order, of anyone who
would try to limit his freedom or his imperious demands. And
each one of us, these stories suggest, harbors a Trickster uncon-
scious that must be brought into awareness and managed, to
save the harm we otherwise will bring and to make constructive
action possible. For freedom without understanding is only
movement and loses the name of action. So Trickster wanders
about instinctively, falling into danger and escaping, bringing
pain to others and himself until he learns to be cunning in his
dealings, and from this careful interest in other people finally
develops a conscience. Whirlwind has given him one more
lesson on his way to becoming fully human, for he has not yet
learned to yield himself to the desires of another, not yet learned
to love.

Mrs. M sat there waiting. "Well, what can you say about
that?" she asked finally.

"He was *stupid!*" Lois said. "He thought he could talk her
into it."

"He wasn't so dumb," Jack said. "At least he had a line. I
liked the way he did that, he wouldn't give up."

"Oh sure, is that how you came on to—well, I won't mention a name." She didn't need to, and Marci looked down at her desk, ignoring the others.

"I don't need a line," Jack said, "I'm sincere"—and the others burst into derisive shouts, delighted.

"They don't call him Grab-ass for nothin," someone said.

"Come on, guys—give me a break."

"He has a point, doesn't he?" Mrs. M said. "If you're interested in someone you're not just coldblooded about it, like Trickster, you have some feelings for the person, don't you?"

"All he wanted was a little fun," Mark said. "So what's wrong with that?"

"Don't be stupid," Lois told him. "The woman said no! But he was trying to get her into the bushes any way he could, that's all he wanted—so she dropped him."

"They'll promise you anything to get what they want," Latasha said. "He was too pushy, he got what he deserved."

"But don't you believe in love at first sight?" Jack said. "He's got to get to know her, doesn't he? How can he do that if she's going to run away? She doesn't give him a chance." He turned to Mrs. M. "What do you say?"

"Well, if a girl gives in to a boy too soon he doesn't learn anything, he can go on being selfish."

"Yeah, make it hard for'em," Latasha said quietly—and those sitting nearby burst out laughing.

"Some girls can be pretty aggressive too, you know," Jack said. "How about that?"

"Don't give in to them too soon, my friend," Mrs. M told him. "You don't want a reputation for being easy, now do you?" And the others laughed again.

"Why do you always favor the girls?"

"I don't really."

No one spoke for a moment, then Leo said "I'll tell you one. There's a guy I know, Joe—from the neighborhood. He's a real nice guy, and he met this girl Anna, who was a real slut, but he really liked her a lot and they started goin out. And then we noticed changes in Joey, like he didn't talk to us anymore. So we didn't like her, and we all kept telling him to watch himself with her, but he wouldn't listen. So one day Joey and

Anna were up in her room, and her parents came home and caught them foolin around. They freaked out, and so she said Joey raped her, and her idiot parents believed her! Joey went to jail for two and a half years—and he only just got out last May. When he came out he saw Anna and he spit in her face and then he left." Leo looked around at the others. "So what do you say about that?"

"That's tough!" Mark said. "He got a bum rap."

"How do you know?" Marci said. "I'll bet there's more to that story."

"I wonder how Anna might tell it," Mrs. M said.

"You sound cynical, you know that?" Mark told her. "I'll bet you've had some experiences. I'll bet you could tell a story."

"I've already told a story today. But there'll be another day."

When the bell sounded the youngsters began to move, reluctantly some of them, lingering there in the dimness talking until the fluorescents flickered on. Mark pushed by me on his way out saying "Watch it, fella!" I was hoping he would have his child well under control after the holiday. He himself was no problem of course, but the child could make trouble for me. I'd be working with him and the rest of this crowd, and I wanted to talk with Mrs. M about them but had to wait until we could meet later in the faculty lunchroom.

As we found places there at a vacant table and put our trays down she said "Well, what did you think of my second period?"

"It was very interesting. But you know, some people would wonder what that had to do with reading and writing."

"But not you, of course." She smiled. "You see, I think there has to be conversation. Everything will come out of that. Reading and writing are only other ways of conversing."

"Yes, but only a few of them were talking."

"That's true, and they all listened. Where else are they going to hear real conversation these days? No wonder the art of conversation is dead, there's hardly anyone who can listen to it. People actually resent someone who has interesting things to say, have you noticed that? They want the attention for themselves."

"I haven't thought about it." But I almost challenged this, she had such an air of self-confident certainty. Her acerbic tone, however, implied that she would brook no opposition so I thought it best to wait. Who else would listen to her talk about her work?

"Besides," she went on, "there's no way you can ever have a general discussion in a class that large. But some of these people have things to say that the others can learn from— there's always a chance something good will be said. I'm willing to take that chance. And you know—I was thinking about this yesterday—there's no public discussion about these things. I mean, boys talk with boys and girls with girls, so they only gossip about each other. What did you think of the story Leo told?"

"He had me interested. You read these stories in the newspaper but you don't think of them happening among the young people you know."

"I told a story about a woman who was justified in what she did to a man, and Leo counters with a story about a woman who was not justified. And did you notice that part about how Joey changed? He didn't talk to the other fellows anymore, he was always with Anna—so they didn't like her. It reminds me of that scene in *Marty* where his friends resent the girl for taking their buddy away. So who knows what really happened between those two? In the war between the sexes the truth gets lost— and we've had this problem right from the beginning, you know. There's a scene in the Navajo creation story when the men desert the women and move across the river, so the women line up along the bank calling to them, then turn their backs and raise their dresses. I'm not sure they improved the view but they made a statement."

"But why did the men leave the women and move across the river?"

"Oh, because the women claimed they were the ones who made everything we need for living in this world, they made life possible. Of course the men resented that challenge. They said 'Well, if you don't need us then live alone and see how you like it'—words to that effect—and they moved away. Of course nobody liked it. After four years the women were hungry for good food and the men were hungry for sex, so they reunited. And it's been an uneasy arrangement ever since, with no end to misunderstanding. Do they talk about these things at the university?

"Oh yes, we talk about communication skills. But I was wondering—did you plan to tell that story about Trickster and Whirlwind today?"

"I was ready in case they gave me that assignment. But I think next time I should have copies of the story ready, and then one of the girls could read Whirlwind's part and a boy could be Trickster. Mark would've been good. I think acting out the story might be more interesting."

"You know, I'm worried about this. I mean, I can't come in here after the holiday and just wait to see what's going to happen like you do, or they'll think I don't know what I'm doing. I'll have to use the textbook." There was a set of composition texts on the shelves under the windows, along with a prose and poetry. "Aren't you supposed to give the principal your lesson plans for the week?"

"Oh I just put down page numbers from the textbook, like everyone else, and that satisfies him. Of course I never open the textbook." She looked at me intently. "Does that bother you? I'm wondering what you will say about me when you go back to the university."

"I'll say that you're a very interesting person."

But she was a puzzle to me at the time. When four years earlier I had sat there as one of her students, events unfolded in a way so natural seeming that after a few days I never wondered about what she was doing. But now I wondered how she managed to control thirty adolescents while so casually provoking them, often with a story. And there were the personal remarks she would make to them. "You're very independent, aren't you?" she told one boy, and he smiled in a self-satisfied way. But he was utterly passive in class, never speaking unless called on and then he would always say "I'm neutral," whatever the subject. "So he always goes his own way," Mrs. M explained, "and that's being very independent. So I'm going to use that. Some day I'll say 'Well, here's someone who always has an independent point of view, let's hear what he says.' And maybe he'll come out of hiding long enough to favor us with a remark." He did—long enough to say "That's about the dumbest damn thing I ever heard!" He was contemptuous, even hostile, and now he was expressing himself. This worried me. Young people bring into the classroom a thousand secrets of pain and humiliation, so that a remark blurted out by one youngster about another, or some inept comment from me, could turn this whole crowd silly or sullen. Learning to teach a lesson here without using their names was going to be difficult enough without experimenting with them as Mrs. M did so often.

And what would have happened if the principal had come in and heard that talk about rape? What if some protective parent became concerned and complained? The year before one had—then another. Their children were being required to read about a prostitute! (In *Crime and Punishment,* which Mrs. M had given to a reading group in one of her classes.) This turned public attention to her other reading assignments, including a short story in which there is the bloody birth of a colt, and to *The Good Earth,* in which the smell of blood is strong as a woman gives birth. "I thought that was the natural way," Mrs. M was said to have remarked. Perhaps the risk of such complaints about reading assignments was one reason she liked to tell young people stories, for spoken words do not linger in the air and she could get away with a story about attempted rape.

Much later it occurred to me that she was very like Trickster herself, because she too enjoyed disturbing the tranquility of routine. If disorder belongs to the totality of life, as Kerényi remarks, then Trickster's role is to give "within the bounds of what is permitted, an experience of what is not permitted"— and Mrs. M liked to question in her casual manner things as they are, raise doubts about ordinary ways of thinking and doing. Much of her strength, it seemed to me, lay in her amused detachment, her ironic attitude toward the entire daily mechanism of the school. She said, "I'll tell you something I usually keep to myself. These young people are going to lead very routine lives, as most of us do, but here in this room life is not always going to be routine. If we're not going to have a good time then I don't want to do it."

Chapter 3

The Economy of Attention

A day is no longer routine when it brings more than our routine share of attention. We want so much to be noticed, to gain some recognition, or otherwise we feel ourselves in deepening shadow, fading away into invisibility. There are few sensations more gratifying than the warm glow of self-satisfaction that comes with receiving one's proper recognition. Yet we are required so often to pay attention rather then receive it—a payment we make with the secret hope that our own turn to collect will come soon and then the light will be ours. But try as they will, some people live as debtors all their lives and must keep making payments, while a lucky few have been born into attention and take it as their natural right, hoping all the while to increase their share. For attention, like wealth, is a commodity always in short supply and no one ever has enough.

Mrs. Martinez, however, did what she could to relieve the shortage, giving attention herself and arranging opportunities for the exchange of it. This caused her some trouble early in her career. The janitor complained that the desks in her room were always out of alignment when he went in to sweep. Those passing by her door heard all the talking and wondered if she ever did any teaching. So one day the principal invited her into his office. Perhaps she was being a little too easy with the students, Dr. Fox said—and too friendly. Her habit of greeting them in the corridors and chatting with them sociably on the school grounds tended to undermine the discipline of the school. "And besides, the boys won't understand, they'll take advantage." He may have had a point there, she thought. "You remember how your friend Jerry Robertson would follow me around after school," she said. "And he called me the Hot Tamale. But I enjoyed talking with you people, I was very curious about you."

She was curious about everyone and would talk with people wherever she went—with taxi drivers, shoe clerks, sometimes even with strangers in the street, and they would tell her things. She had a way of giving them the attention that would draw something from them. One time as we went into her local hardware store a middle-aged man standing there offered to help, and she told him what she wanted, saying she wasn't very handy with things, and they went down a narrow aisle between high shelving. "If you need anything else," he said, reaching into a bin, "you better get it today because I won't be here tomorrow." He spoke with a Caribbean accent, in liquid vowels.

"I'm glad you told me," she said, "because I like doing business with you. You're always very patient and very helpful."

He held his hands out before him waist-high, palms up, saying "You see these hands? These hands are blessed."

"Oh—why is that?"

"You see, when I was eighteen in Grenada I started building a house, all by myself, with these hands. And when I was twenty-one the house was finished—and I did it all by myself, with these hands. And then I got married. These hands brought me my wife! Then after a while we rented out the house—it must be worth a hundred thousand dollars now—and we left Grenada and came to the States. So then I went to school to study computer programming, and I got a job working with a computer. But I didn't like it. These hands could do it but it wasn't with the people. So when my friends bought this store with all these tools I came to work here, so I could be with the people. These hands are blessed."

He must have been thinking about this for a long time, he had those thoughts ready and he gave them to her. Why? Was it because she would listen to people, give them attention—was that why they were willing to reveal themselves like this? Or does being a woman make a difference? Perhaps men are willing to confide in a woman. As we were leaving, I said "Why did he tell you that, I wonder?" "When we came in I saw him looking at his hands." I still didn't understand it.

But it must be easier for women to gather secrets like this, I thought—they've learned to give a willing ear while men talk on about themselves. So often in restaurants, on the street, in school corridors, we can see a woman inclining her head attentively toward some man whose mouth is working, and we can see that she knows exactly what she is doing. She is giving the attentive support his sensitive ego requires, concealing her impatience or boredom while he expresses himself at length. Her self-denial is the consequence of long experience—in classrooms, for example, where from first grade through college the boys speak out three times as often as the girls and are given five times as much attention by their teacher. When the teacher is female they are even more favored! So women learn to subordinate their own need for attention to male prerogatives—and their reward for this may be the entertaining and even useful stories they hear. Listening has become essentially a feminine skill.

So I said, "The reason people tell you these things is because you're a woman—isn't that it?" We were sitting in a corner of the faculty room, where now as one of the teaching staff I felt quite at home. I had come back to this school partly because Mrs. M was still there and I was willing to be her apprentice in order to learn a few things that are not in the books. And I wondered how she managed to continue on her eccentric way in this rather traditional school.

She glanced over at me, amused. "It's easier for me to get a story from a man, of course, but women have good things to say too. You must have found that out by now."

"But you're willing to listen to them, isn't that it? Being a woman that must come more easily to you. No one is telling me these stories."

"Well, actually I learned this from my father." While she was growing up she saw that all kinds of people would reveal themselves to him. He had a gift, it seemed. And he was a great womanizer—that was the first thing she noticed, how the women loved him. About women he had endless curiosity, he was willing to listen to them by the hour. When his business associates asked him to explain how he was so successful in his love affairs, he said "Gentlemen, if we spent as little time with our business as we do with our women, where would our business be?" He was willing to give them attention.

"But he wanted something from them," I said. "That's why he would listen—he was sexually interested. In a way he was taking advantage."

"Of course there's a sexual interest! There always is when men and women are talking—and I intend to take full advantage of that. The fact that you and I are not of the same sex adds a certain piquancy to our conversation, even though I'm older than you—don't you think?"

"Alright—but he was a womanizer, he wanted something from them."

"Yes, and what he really wanted was a remembrance to take away. He would talk to any woman anywhere. 'A Campbell never met a woman he didn't like'—that was his motto. He'd say that and laugh. But men liked talking with him too because he did not compete with them for attention, he would listen. I think a man would rather have another man's attention than a woman's, because women are not that important. So my father would give other men his attention, he would draw them out. He was interested in people. One time he asked a new business acquaintance what the son was doing, and tears came to the man's eyes, then he started crying—because the son had got married the week before. And he had not invited his father to the wedding! Or even mentioned it. When that boy was growing up his father had no time for him, he was too busy with business and the son learned to live without him. If you want to be loved you had better give attention—that was my father's comment."

"So that's it," I said, reaching for my books, getting ready to leave for my next class. "You have to be willing to listen to people."

"No—it's what comes before the listening that matters." We went out into the crowded corridor. I was still puzzled.

And there was something troubling about her claim to have learned this from her father. His success in business must have greatly increased the value of his ear: he was someone worth talking to. And his listening would in fact affirm his standing in the community, just as doctors or lawyers giving their clients attention affirm their superior status. So there may have been no particular skill in what he did. But Mrs. M occupied a much lower social position, since a teacher is no more than a low-level civil servant, and her ear would be of little value. She must have consciously developed the skill of drawing people out, so that despite her lack of social position or power they still valued her attention—and that gave her a certain power. For one thing, it gave her time while the other person was talking to prepare a telling remark. But how did she manage to gain this influence?

As we sat down in our usual corner in the faculty room, Vitaly got up and came over to us. He'd been sitting on the sofa with Hennessey talking about basketball but now there was something else on his mind. "I got this paper yesterday," he told Mrs. M, leafing through a thick stack of student compositions, looking for it. "They were writing about their hopes and dreams, and look at this!" He held it out to her, indicating a passage: "What I want most of all is to see vultures eating my father's GUTS." Mrs. M said, "Well, you got something out of her."

"I took it to her guidance counselor," Vitaly said. "This girl needs help, she has problems. And he said I shouldn't show it to him. He said there's nothing we can do, and if we did and something happened we could get sued. I thought at least somebody ought to talk with her." He was speaking rapidly, he was upset.

"Maybe just writing about it helped her," Mrs. M said.

"No one else wrote anything personal. They wrote about getting a car and going to college and making money. But this one upsets me."

"You know, Vitaly, I always see you carrying around a stack of papers. And you write comments on them all, don't you? You work very hard."

"Yes," he said, taking out his pipe, "I spent last night reading these. If you make them write then you owe it to them to read the papers—that's how I feel about it. I told my wife when we got married, my students come first, then her. It took her awhile to understand that but now she accepts it." He lit the pipe, looking pleased with himself.

"I can't work as hard as you do," Mrs. M remarked. "I won't spend my evenings reading papers."

Vitaly looked at her thoughtfully, puffing out some smoke. Then he said, "I have a confession. I went by your room yesterday and I spied on you, I looked through the little window in your door. You were all sitting in a circle and talking. But I can't teach that way, I have to have them in front of me, I have to be sure everyone is paying attention. I have things to tell them."

"Well I guess that's the difference—I don't have anything to tell them." Vitaly looked uncertain for a moment, as though he wondered if she were gibing him.

After he had left us I said "Vitaly is so professorial—he lectures in class all the time. He has a pipe-smoking air of astuteness."

"And I like him!" she was quick to say. "He'd rather sit here and talk teaching with us than sit over there talking basketball. And he works very hard, he believes in what he's doing. I respect him. But I wouldn't want to be married to him."

There was some attraction there certainly, because he kept coming back to her and she seemed to enjoy listening to him talk about his work. Then one day she made a suggestion that got him into trouble. During lunch he began talking about *Huckleberry Finn*: "It's a picaresque novel, and I think I should explain that to the class. I want them to be ready for it." He looked at us but we had nothing to say. After a moment he turned to Mrs. M. "What would you do with it?"

She glanced away, thinking about this. "Well, I've never taught *Huckleberry Finn*. I suppose we could start reading the book right there in class, and you could ask them to come in the next day with something in the story they want to point out to the others, something they like or don't like or want to ask about. Then we organize into small groups and share with each other what we've found. We could try that and see what happens. Maybe they'll ask you about something, and then you can talk."

He was thinking it over. "If it doesn't work I can always go back to my lecture."

"You're free to do whatever you want." But she had already told me that once you start down this road it may be difficult to turn back, the youngsters want to keep on talking. So Vitaly would be taking more of a chance than he realized, having been listened into it over a long time by Mrs. M, who wasn't one to worry about dangers along the way. At least he would have in her the comfort of a traveling companion, even if neither one knew where he was going. I was looking forward to hearing his report.

A few days later he was with us in the faculty room again, sitting on the edge of his chair and leaning forward, giving a complete account that ended with "So they really talked! One of them even stood up and argued with somebody across the room. The best discussion we've had all year! And it was the black students who carried it. But they think it's a racist book, they don't like that word 'nigger.' " He looked anxious. "I don't want a riot in there." And something else was bothering him. Three youngsters, the ones who would always raise their hands, had sat silently the whole time, looking sullen. Vitaly was worried.

Mrs. M said, "Well, there will always be some who won't take part, but you have most of them with you, they're interested in what you're doing. Sounds good to me. Maybe I should send Marvin to your class, he's not doing anything in mine. One paper, that's all he's done this year—about basketball of course. But it was interesting. He said the team does a lot of traveling, and after a game the girls come crowding around the locker room door waiting for the players to come out, and they shout the numbers of the boys they want to meet, like 'Hey, Lucky Eleven!'—that's Marvin's number. He's met a lot of friendly girls on those trips. With all that attention coming to him, why work for me? I tell him, 'Marvin, you've got the goods, so why not let us see it?' I have to compete with those girls and the coach for his virility."

Two days later Dr. Fox called Vitaly into his office. Three students had complained that his class was all talk, that no teaching was going on. And furthermore, Dr. Fox had received two phone calls from parents who complained that *Huckleberry Finn* is a racist book. "That book has been in the curriculum for years and we've never had any trouble with it before," Dr. Fox told him. Then he came the next day to visit Vitaly's classroom, and seeing the youngsters sitting in their study groups reading and talking, he said "I'll come back when you're teaching."

"Oh, I feel like a failure!" Vitaly told us, genuinely distressed. "I feel I'm not a real teacher. My Slavic soul is suffering!"

"It's not easy to work with young people," Mrs. M said. "So much can happen."

"Yes, so I go back to the book, to quiet. I want them to see it, I want to tell them. They don't understand it! When I was growing up no black people were there, I never saw one, but every year I go down the river on the raft with Jim so now I know we're friends. But my brother, he grew up suspicious." Having said all this very rapidly, he fumbled now in his jacket pocket for his pipe.

"So you're out on the river with those youngsters," Mrs. M was saying, "you're having an experience with them."

"But we drift!" He had found the pipe, but then he put it back in his pocket. "I don't know what to do. I think about my lecture."

"Well, it's not easy for some of them to go along with you and Huck on the raft. They feel too dependent, maybe. If we keep listening to them, then we'll know what they're thinking."

"But they complain to Dr. Fox, they say I'm not teaching, all we do is talk!"

"Oh we know who complained," Mrs. M told him. "Your three hand-wavers, I'd say. They're unhappy because now they don't get all your attention, they have to share it, so they went behind your back to get what they think is rightly theirs. Don't worry about them, you have the rest of the class with you."

Much later, while I was thinking about this, it occurred to me those three were unhappy because the threat to them ran even deeper than the loss of their special status. During the time when individuals in that classroom were expected to take the initiative entirely on their own behalf, without regard for others, they had won the approbation of their teacher, they had answered his questions. But as Vitaly moved toward making the allocation of attention cooperative and mutually supportive, rather than competitive, they were called upon to negotiate their ideas with others, who could now bring into play their experiences and social skills. Those three may have felt themselves falling then back into the general mass—or perhaps entering into a situation even more competitive than before, when they really had no competition but rather cooperated with their teacher in reminding others of their inferior status and keeping them invisible. But that was an irony I hardly recognized at the time.

And unlike Vitaly, I was only a spectator of the game Mrs. Martinez played, I was avoiding trouble. He sat down with us at lunch the next day, still shaken. "I think I should go talk to Dr. Fox," he told us. "I want him to understand what I'm doing."

"Yes, he should understand what you're doing," Mrs. M agreed. "So you go to his office and he'll sit back and listen while you defend yourself, then he'll tell you to get that class back to work. Remember, Vitaly, the one who is listening is the one who has control! So don't defend yourself, don't surrender control of what you're doing. *You* are the authority in that classroom, not Dr. Fox. He was a basketball coach, you know. The next time he comes in to visit your class, you invite him to sit down and take part. You're in charge there!"

Vitaly fumbled nervously with his pipe. It seemed to me that perhaps she had done him no favor, considering the distress her advice had brought him. I myself was staying close to the textbook. There were two of them, a prose and poetry that Mrs. M used occasionally, and a composition-grammar that she had abandoned long ago. As a likable eccentric who brought some variety to a routine day she had license, she could get away with it—but perhaps a school can tolerate only one Mrs. Martinez. I certainly did not want any quizzical attention from Dr. Fox. When, I wondered, would he next favor Vitaly with another visit?

But Dr. Fox had something else in mind for him, something that would take care of several problems. At a meeting of the entire faculty in the cafeteria he instructed us in Learning by Objectives, while we responded much as students do everywhere. A few raised their hands for attention and asked questions, while others prayed they would shut up and let the meeting end. The faculty-room bridge players sat together looking as if they wished someone had remembered to bring a deck of cards, their hands restless. The coaching staff, soon satisfied that none of this concerned them, began snickering among themselves. Notes were passed. Dr. Fox was explaining that we were to prepare a list of specific objectives for each subject area, and then the progress of our students could be evaluated in terms of those objectives. Just as any well-run business has its goals, so should we.

A few doubts about all this were expressed, a few objections raised, then Dr. Fox went on to appoint the committees that would coordinate the work of writing objectives. Vitaly was named to chair the committee for junior and senior English. It was not an honor he welcomed.

"I don't see myself a businessman," he told us indignantly, "I see myself an artist! Some work in different mediums—you sculpt, you paint, and what I do, I take these kids from out there and I shape them into students. I don't say intellectuals, because of course I don't do that, but I prepare them to be students, so in a sense I'm an artist. These objectives are for math teachers, science teachers, not for us."

"Yes, but we ought to have some result in mind," Mrs. M said.

"A technician, yes, with a blueprint," Vitaly told her excitedly, "but an artist, no! He starts out, he has his medium, like I take these children as my medium and I don't know what will happen with them. Don't you see? It's like when you make a story and you don't know what will be coming until it's finished. Don't you see?"

"Well, if I understand this, you're saying that we learn what we can do with children as we go along, is that it?"

"Yes! Objectives, who needs them? They come last!"

"You know, I think that's right. Listing objectives is a technician's way of organizing instruction, not a poet's."

"But *you*—" he was stiff with indignation. "You said we could do this! You supported him!"

It was true. When in the meeting objections were coming one after another, the opposition gathering strength, Mrs. M had stood up and said that after all, we could do this easily—and then we would have statements of purpose the community would understand. After that the opposition faded away. "Yes," she agreed, "I did support him. He's kept me here all these years, and he's let me alone. We understand each other. English and basketball are much alike."

I wondered if she was being serious or was she trying to provoke him? Vitaly said, "But it's a matter of principle! We have to stand up for what we know is right!"

"Well, I'd rather stand up for a person than a principle. If we—"

"But you don't stand up for *me!* I raise questions and other people support me, not you!"

"My friend, everyone in the class enjoys it when someone gives the teacher a hard time, so they encourage you. They like to see Dr. Fox under fire. But the truth is, they're very comfortable here with things as they are. Before long you would find yourself out in front carrying the banner alone—and I'd like to see you last here another year at least."

Vitaly was shifting nervously in his seat, eager to speak, full of fight. "But he's only a coach, you said yourself, so how can he tell me how to teach *Huckleberry Finn?*"

"He won't. And if anyone questions what you're doing, you point to that list of objectives. You can use it to justify anything you want to do. If you want to teach *Huckleberry Finn* as a picaresque novel, then go right ahead—just put that on your list. That's what those committees will do, they'll take objectives out of the textbooks and then we'll write a few new exams, and everything will go on just as before. Nothing will change! If you want to kill this thing quickly, then embrace it."

Vitaly opened his mouth, closed it, then pulled his pipe out of his pocket. "And by the way," Mrs. M continued, "Dr. Fox didn't think this up by himself, he's only doing what the central office tells him. And we have to support him, we have to help him look good. If he's ever going to learn anything from us, then he has to feel that we are with him. After all, who is going to teach him if we don't?"

"Then we should talk to Dr. Fox, he needs to understand. He should know that English is poetry, not science, not business!"

"Yes, you're right—we teach an untidy subject. So let's tell Dr. Fox all this, and he will sit back listening to us, he'll nod, and then he will tell us to go write the objectives. Remember—the one who listens is the one who has control."

"You keep saying that, but no! Dr. Fox, he has control in his office and I have control in my classroom, they are to learn from me!"

"Yes, in your classroom you have the power, so you can talk all you want to. And the children sitting there, they can listen if they want to, or they can think about something else, they can sleep with their eyes open. They have control. You see," and here she leaned toward him, "in my classroom I intend to have control." There's something very calculating about this woman, I thought.

Vitaly was digging nervously into the bowl of his pipe with a small tool. "You agree but you don't agree," he said.

"Well, maybe that's because I don't know what I'm doing. I just go to those meetings to get my instructions, not to argue decisions with Dr. Fox. Do we really need Father's attention that much?" Why would we, I thought, when we have Mother's? "You know," she continued, "he put you in charge of that committee to see if you will work with him. So work with him, my friend, and keep listening. You're not going to be in this school very long, either of you. I don't know where you'll go," she had turned to me, "but our scholar here will be teaching in a college before long. When you two are gone I'll be here alone."

Thinking about this conversation later I realized that over a long period she had listened to Vitaly in order to prepare his receptivity for the moment when she would confide a few thoughts to him. Our Mrs. M was certainly not the born teacher so praised in legend, moved spontaneously by a noble soul, she was calculating—her skills had been acquired, she knew exactly what she was doing. Her attitude was that of a professional, as though like a doctor or lawyer or consulting engineer she were being paid to listen, and doing so she maintained a sense of being apart from, even above the events around her. A person talking is caught up in the immediate moment, engrossed in a presentation of self, whereas the one listening—really listening, that is, and not merely waiting for a turn to speak—may have an ironic distance on the exchange. Mrs. M enjoyed exploring the discrepant situation in which she worked, the gap between its reality and its public rhetoric, and in that gap she found her place.

Operating from this location she saw contradictions being lived all around us, and she would sometimes point them out— although how she could get away with the provocative remarks she sometimes made was puzzling to me. When one day I went to meet her after school she was sitting in the back of her room with Marvin, who slouched at his desk, a baseball cap on his head. She was speaking very quietly, with an effect on him so marked that later I asked her what was said. "Now my friend," she told him, "you never mix with us. You sit here in the back, and when we help each other you never take anyone's paper, you never give help. I wonder why?"

Marvin was looking down at his feet. "I like keepin to myself."

"Well, you're really aggressive and pushy on the basketball court, you're hell on rubber out there, right?"

He was grinning, nodding, yeah yeah!

"So tell me something. Is that what keeps you in school, playing basketball? Is that it? What will you do next year?"

"I'm gonna college," he said. "Basketball don' last, I know that. So I'm gonna be in a office, make money."

"Well my friend, the honkies are going to *love* you in that office! You're going to be sitting there in the back somewhere, not pushing your way in—and that's what they want. So you better start getting pushy, my friend. You're intelligent, so"— and here she leaned toward him—"don't come shufflin in here playin dumb on my team! Show us what you got!"

He was frozen there for a moment, his face impassive. Then he unfolded himself and stood over her, six feet two. "You some momma," he said. That was a compliment and he went out, staring me down as he passed. I wasn't about to try anything like that. Somehow she managed to prepare a path for the remark about to come, so that even as it startled it felt right.

But those were rare occasions, gaining all the more force for their rarity since she spoke very little even in her classroom, preferring to draw out the experience of others and remarking the ironic turns in their lives, all the more ironic for being expressed unawares. One day she brought this paper to the lunch table:

poor woman's pride

My sister Carla started dating Tony when she was seventeen. They both worked in the pizza parlor on Front Street, and Tony was twenty-one. When they started going out my family was worried, especially my mother and my brother. They thought Tony was too old for her. They told her he'd never get anywhere, he was nothing but a ragazzo from Naples, he didn't even graduate from high school. They told her she couldn't see him anymore. But Carla continued to see Tony, and finally the family decided to accept the relationship thinking it wouldn't last. Then when they got to know Tony they liked him. Except my mother, she still didn't like him.

Carla went to college and the family was relieved that she wouldn't give up her education for Tony, but he encouraged her to go to school and do well. By the time she graduated Tony had gone to Phoenix. He looked all over the U.S. to find a city that needed a good New York pizza parlor, and he decided that Phoenix was the place. He opened his restaurant and it was doing well. His good fortune was just beginning.

One night Carla came home and said that she was moving to Phoenix. The family was really upset. Then she said that she had landed a management job in a big department store there, and they felt better. So Carla went to Phoenix, to be with Tony.

His pizza business was doing very well. He paid off his loan and he opened another restaurant. He paid off the loan on that one in about a year, and he began saving money to open another restaurant. But then he decided to invest the money he had saved, and he sold the two restaurants for $900,000. By now even my mother liked Tony. Not because of the money, but because of the way he handled it.

On Carla's 24th birthday Tony asked her to marry him. She said yes, but she was beginning to change. She was growing resentful of Tony's money, gained from work that required no education. She was working all day and she went to school at night, but Tony could take trips to Acapulco. She got behind in her rent and he offered to help out, but she was proud and wouldn't let him. She got behind in her car payments and he offered to buy her the car but she wouldn't let him. They finally broke up on Valentine's Day. Sometimes two people have dreams that do not go together.

What had Mrs. M done to elicit this story, I wondered. There had been an argument in her class, something about what kind of man does a young woman want, and she had given them Nelson Algren's story "poor man's pennies." Gladys, who could have her choice of the single men in her Chicago neighborhood, chooses Sobotnik—a little man, a petty thief, a liar. And when people wonder why, when they tell her he's only a liar, she answers "Lies are a poor man's pennies." She is determined to make a decent human being of him, and she finally succeeds. It's an ironic story that reveals the truth about a man through his lies, and in which a woman who appears to be sacrificing herself for the good of another is actually assuming the dominant role in their relationship. Mrs. M had asked her youngsters to write their reactions to this story and then go on to tell about couples they knew themselves. And so Dora had written "poor woman's pride."

It makes an ironic contrast with "poor man's pennies." Here are two independent women who choose men others think of as losers, and they hold to those men without the support of family or friends. Each sees in her man something others do not, she sees his possibility. And what's more, she sees an opportunity to gain attentive deference for herself. Secure in the knowledge that she is superior to the man she has chosen, each woman expects to hold the dominant place. Gladys could not be satisfied with a man who wants her to follow and serve, but with Sobotnik she commands his grateful attention. And Carla, who is educated well beyond Tony, can expect that he will admire her achievements and listen to her. These women want to both nurture a man and dominate him, as mothers do their children. And Gladys takes an almost professional attitude toward Sobotnik: if she can make a competent man of him, then she is a success. But Carla has a different idea of success: she must achieve recognition outside her marriage and command the attention not just of one man but of other people as well. And for that attention she finds herself in competition with

Tony. In the end her self-regard, her pride, will not allow her to marry a man who has surpassed her—because after all he may be rich but he doesn't know anything! He's not good enough for her, just as mother and brother told her in the beginning. Although by now of course they have come to regard Tony very differently.

For seven years Carla had relied on the fact that her education would exert a powerful claim on the attention of others, independently of her income or occupational status. Those who speak in the accents of the educated are going to be taken more seriously than those whose speech reveals a lack of learning, for education suggests the possession of intelligence and of specialized knowledge. And so a casual remark about one's degree, or the dropping of a bit of specialized knowledge, often serves to secure respectful consideration for whatever one is saying. Here Carla had a great advantage over Tony and surely expected to receive in their social interactions with others the greater share of attention. But his new wealth overshadowed that advantage and she felt diminished by it, only half-visible in the penumbra it cast. Wealth always brings its possessor into the warm glow of respectful attention.

Tony has lived the classic American success story and become the self-made man. In a culture where male worth is usually contingent on economic achievement, he has by his competitive effort, alone, proved himself worthy. He has established his right to be listened to when the conversation begins. But now women too are becoming competitive and self-oriented, more willing to accept as legitimate the same narcissistic attention-getting behavior as the male. Tony may have encouraged Carla to become independent but he also offered to support her—and this must have been a great temptation, one she had to reject along with Tony himself, for she too would be self-made. And her rejection of Tony on Valentine's Day, a day for declaring your love, must have shaken his self-confidence. Somehow his success had brought him a defeat.

Dora had watched during those seven years with fascinated attention her sister's unfolding romance, with all its multiple ironies. And now she was willing, even eager, to share the story with Mrs. M and allow her to use it with other classes. So this was one way to manage without a textbook. But what did Dora think of her sister's rejection of Tony, I wondered—how did she understand it? "Did you ask Dora what she thought about this?"

"She said that all Tony had going for him was his money."

"And what did you say?"

"Oh, I agreed with her."

Dora, then, knew this romance as her sister had lived it within the flow of event—and rather than either woman mastering the irony of the situation, it seems, the irony had mastered her. Feelings change, things happen, and then reasons must be found to justify what happens and preserve the illusion that we know what we are doing. Carla may very well have made the right decision, but if she did so without any perception of the ironic situation in which she lived, then it can hardly be said she made a decision at all. For irony is the mastered moment, as the philosopher says, and makes decisiveness possible.

Yet Mrs. M had agreed with Dora. I was beginning to understand that she was herself an ironist, whose satisfactions are enjoyed in silence and whose concern is that no one notice her deceptions. But now *I* had noticed, and felt as though I had discovered a undercover agent living among us and gathering secrets no one knew were there, all for some purpose of her own. Sharing her experience with Vitaly and me, she seemed to open herself receptively, and with her I felt free and expansive—yet at the same time drawn unwillingly under her power, both attracted and repulsed, disoriented somehow in those familiar surroundings by her ironic moves.

She advised me once to be less argumentative, to stop saying "Yes, but"—unless of course, she added, "you want to goad someone into developing a thought you already agree with." I was too surprised by this to respond, even with yes, but—I needed time to think about it. By disagreeing, I suppose, you strengthen the other person's commitment to your own position. And then after your opponent, who is really your colleague but doesn't know it, has been inspired by your opposition to feats of imaginative argument and has built a strong case for your own view, you can allow yourself to accept, reluctantly, the position so persuasively set forth. Mrs. M had found a practical use for irony. And the ironist is a "vampire who has sucked the blood out of her lover and fanned him with coolness, lulled him to sleep and tormented him with turbulent dreams" (Kierkegaard).

So of course she had to do her work secretly without drawing too much attention herself. Rather, she would exploit in various ways the need everyone around her felt for attention and recognition—particularly the need of those young people sent to her year after year. Most young people spend their days in a segregated children's world where the adults who supervise them have little time to give each child attention, and so they must compete constantly with each other for recognition from parent or teacher or coach. After a time some may succeed while others give up the competition and withdraw, resigning themselves to invisibility—although withdrawal may itself be a bid for attention. By one means or another young people must strive to elicit the regard that testifies to their individual worth. In fact, their sense of being independent individuals develops along with the anxious feeling that they have their existence as persons only in the regard that others give them, and so they are not really independent after all. They come, that is, to self-awareness within an economy of attention—and a few of them, for a short time each day, for only a year, lived within an economy managed by Mrs. Martinez. And because of her ironic art they hardly knew what was happening to them.

The more time we spent together the more perplexing she seemed, until the thought occurred to me that I hardly knew anything about her. So while we were considering the puzzle of Carla and Tony's affair, I said "You've had a romance too. I'm wondering how you met your husband."

She hesitated, glancing at me. "I'm not sure you would understand if I told you that story."

"Try me—I'm learning to listen."

"Well, it begins with a death and ends with dancing. I first saw the man who would become my husband at a funeral near Sunrise Lodge, and my attention kept wandering from the service to him. Someone said he came from a long way off, but from where and who he was no one seemed to know. The mystery was intriguing. We could hear drumbeats during the service, and as we walked away afterwards we saw a gathering of

Navajos nearby. This was unusual enough to draw us over there because Navajos will not gather for a funeral. For them it's too late, the worst has happened, they should have been told earlier—but now their friend the trader's wife was gone, so that was something to talk about, so they were gathering. Slim Fingers was beating the drum. This was the beginning of a ceremony, the Prostitutionway, a charm against excess in life and love, and it begins with a dance we called the sweetie sweetie. A girl goes up to the man of her choice and touches him. If he dances with her he must pay a dollar. If he does not dance with her he pays the dollar. Whatever his decision he is going to pay for it. So I went up to the stranger and touched him, but he shook his head no and reached into his pocket for the dollar. So then I pulled the jacket from his hand—he had it slung over his shoulder—and danced away. Among my people women can be very aggressive, and when a woman takes something that belongs to a man she is making a very definite suggestion, and the man must agree or give up his property. He danced with me then, and that is how I met my husband in that good day."

This story was like a gift to me, she so rarely talked about herself, and I was pleased to have it. There is a certain pleasure in being the one favored with some long-felt and perhaps heretofore secret reminiscence that reveals the life in someone who has been only another element in the daily routine. This was a pleasure Mrs. M often enjoyed—for it was not her way to watch and wonder about someone from a distance, but rather she had from the beginning an aggressive interest in others and, modified by art, it brought her many gifts.

Another time, much later, we were together in Manhattan and walking down through a long tunnel to the PATH train on our way to Jersey City. As we came out onto the platform we saw a man there alone, pushing a broom and singing. Mrs. M breezed through the turnstile calling out "Sing to me! Sing to me!" and went up to him. "Ah," he said "I jist come in from Dublin this verra mornin, an now I'm to clean this station an go on to Hoboken an sweep there. I'm tired!"

"Well," she said "when ya work fer the IRA it sure keeps ya hoppin"—and he burst into song again:

Say what wind from the south
Brings a messenger here
With a hymn for the dawn
Of the free.

A train was coming into the station, slowing down, but she turned back to say "You like to sing."

"It's my comfort." We stepped into a car and the doors slid shut.

As we sat down in the long row of seats along one side, I said "You haven't lost your touch."

"No, but soon I'll be too old. When people think I'm no longer sexually active, then my attention won't be worth their time. They'll think of me as already lifeless. I'll be that little old lady sitting next to you in the bus or the plane asking questions, and you won't want to talk. Only children will talk to me then."

Somehow I found this hard to believe. She turned to a young man sitting beside her, a suitcase on the floor between his feet and a canvas bag on his lap. "Running away from home?" she asked.

Chapter 4

When Time Is Broke

Those who control our time control our lives, binding us to schedules and regular obligations, imposing on us a moral standard so that we are judged lazy or ambitious, serious or frivolous, worthy or unworthy, according to the way we use our time. Authority is fused with the clock. And the dissenter who wanders from the compelling path of time will be severely punished, so that in the end fear—of losing a job, perhaps, or failing a grade—compels submission to the clock. Fear and the implicit promise that a future will be secured if only everyone learns to be on time.

And the little time remaining to us in the day, the unbound time, is free for empathy and love. But all relationships in our culture have a temporal dimension, so that as we wait for the one who finally arrives and later leaves, we not only perceive time but feel it. Anxiety, anger, and love may all be expressed by the simple question, *When?* The empathetic use of time, bringing us into rhythm with others as we move to the same emotional pulse, creates whatever social harmony we will know in the course of a day, or night. So empathy may create its own temporal order, and fear may compel submission to a timetable—and which of these shall move the classroom clock?

When Sheree came late into the second period class, closing the door carefully and soft-footing her way down the aisle, Mrs. M turned and said "Just a moment my friends, let me ask this late-coming lady what she has for us."

"But it's not my fault! I shouldna hafta do nothin!"

"Oh, I *know* there's a good reason, but what do you have for us?" The door opened again and Dan came in.

"See, I'm not the only one! It's not fair!" She dropped her books onto a desk and sat down defiantly, folding her arms across her chest and looking around the room for support. "It's not fair!" But the others were smiling and waiting, enjoying this. She was an angry seventeen-year-old, slender and dark. "Oh alright, I got a wise saying. Don't you argue with Dr. Fox, ya can't never win. So there!" She sat stiffly, arms still folded, staring ahead.

"That's excellent advice, and we thank you. Now—"

"He stop me in the hall," Sheree said. "He askin why you not in school first period? So what's it to'im, I wanna know."

"Well, that's between you and him. Now let me ask this late-coming gentleman what he has for us."

Dan had shuffled slowly along the aisle toward his seat—tall, heavyset and Irish, wearing a torn black T-shirt and baggy jeans. "I suppose you know I got a good reason," he said.

"I'm sure you do. But what do you have for us?"

"I got a poem. Ya wanna hear it?" And he began to recite: "Evil ideas and thoughts unwind / As the fire begins to spread / No one knows why it started / Everyone knows the dread / Mass confusion and destruction / Spread throughout the land / As your frightened families / All pray hand in hand."

He nodded to a scattering of applause, and Mrs. M said "That's very interesting—what is it?"

"Just another song I wrote for the band." He sang with a local rock band, practicing in a dingy basement and doing an occasional local gig.

"I'll need a copy of that for the minutes," Rosalie told him, so Dan pulled a folded piece of paper from his pocket and sent it to her across the room by a chain of passing hands. He'd come prepared.

It seemed to me that all this delayed the start of work, and since the class period was only forty-five minutes long, every minute counted. She could have begun the lesson immediately and taken care of the delinquents later as they tried to slip away at the end of the period hoping she'd forgotten about them—but starting on time was obviously not much of a concern with her.

Why was she encouraging all this diversion? I needed to

know, I was there to study her work and explain to the doctoral seminar just how she used the forty-five minutes of the instructional period. What were her aims or objectives, and how did she go about achieving them? I was expected to give a well-organized, expository account demonstrating the logic of her teaching practice—but it wasn't logical, the woman seemed to be making it up as she went along. "What I need are activities and good things to read, not objectives," she told me. "I'll find out what I'm doing after we've done it. 'The poem finds its own name as it goes'—you remember that line?" And yet, if I couldn't find a logic in her work to organize my description of it, I'd have to report it anecdotally or in a story—and would that do for a doctoral seminar?

When we sat down together for lunch later in the day, I said "So you make everyone who comes late to class say something, is that it? But doesn't that delay the lesson?"

"What lesson?"

I was nonplused for a moment and she glanced at me, amused. "Only joking," she said, although I realized later that in fact she had not taught a lesson in any formal sense that day. "No, I don't make them do that, the group does. People who come late break our rhythm, so they owe us something—and the class decided they should give us a poem or a wise saying. If I don't call on them, then the secretary will at the end of the period, but today I thought Sheree and Dan needed to speak. Most people would rather be on time than perform. Except Dan. He came late deliberately so he could try his lyric on us."

"But doesn't that mean they bring a lot of distractions into the class?"

"I hope so." She was trying to provoke me, I thought. "They have other interests than school," she continued, "and I have to find some way to bring those into the room so we can use them. And besides, people are going to be late whatever you do, so I use that. Do you remember the fable Kafka told about the tribe that paid homage to its god by laying a sacrifice of fresh meat on the altar, and one day a leopard leaped out from the jungle and took it? A ferocious beast. And when the leopard appeared at the next sacrifice and snatched away the offering, and again at the next, the tribe finally made that part of the ritual. So that's what I do. Rather than punish them for being late, I incorporate that into our ritual. Now I'm waiting to see if my other classes hear about this and want to try it."

A loud bell announced the end of the period, and we got up from the table. "You know," she said, "I enjoy these conversations we have. You make me think up reasons for what I do."

What she did, it seemed to me, was invent the program as she went along, improvising from one day to the next, relying for direction on the fortuitous turn of event. She had stories to read with them, and poems, and she would bring in other materials from time to time, so she had a pattern of sorts in one reading after another, but did she have any specific learning goals in mind for her young people? Across the top of a chalkboard at the front of her room was written "Objective: To understand that language makes thought possible." I had seen that up there every day for some weeks, so finally I said "That objective you have on the board—it's the same one every day for every class."

"Oh yes, it never wears out." It was there, she explained, in case the assistant principal came to observe or the English supervisor looked in. Protective camouflage. Every lesson she taught was supposed to begin with a statement of a learning objective, continue with instructional activities to achieve it, then end with a restatement and evaluation of progress. The new superintendent of schools had read a book, *Learn Faster—Learn More!*, and that slogan appealed to him so now every lesson would begin with a point and *stay with that point!*

"So I give them what they want," she said, "I give them an objective. After all, anything we do here demonstrates that language makes thought possible. You see, I've been through all this before. Every few years someone comes along with another system for controlling our time in the name of efficiency. Long ago there was Planned Program Budgeting, and then came Learning by Objectives—when you were teaching here, remember?—and now we have TEL, which means Teaching Effective Lessons. The technicians are in charge, of course, not the poets. So if you want to live here that means a little subterfuge now and then." She turned to move off down the corridor, looking back to say "Keep it to yourself." She had a way of making one feel like a co-conspirator.

When I went to visit her class the next day she began by passing out sheets of paper and asking the youngsters, apropos of nothing at all it seemed, to supply couplets to make a poem. "If my Irish friend here can do it," she said, indicating Dan, "then we can do it. I'm feeling generous today, so I'll supply the paper if you will supply the lines. Just follow this pattern and write as many lines as you can. We'll see what we get." On the board she had written the line starters "I used to . . . / Now I . . ."—which I recognized as an exercise devised by the poet Kenneth Koch for his work with young children. "My best ideas are the ones I've stolen," she told me once, but if so she certainly gave them a twist of her own.

"Why we gotta do this?" Dan asked. "What's the point?"

"I don't know yet," she said, sitting down at her desk to write. "But you're a poet so I'm surprised you're asking me that. Let's try this and see what happens. You don't have to think about it, just put down whatever comes to you."

And most of them began writing. I was surprised there wasn't more resistance to this, as there would have been if I'd asked such a group to improvise a few lines. There were more minority and underclass youngsters here than when I was a student in this school, and they could be a restless crowd. But today even those who weren't writing sat there quietly at least—except for Letty in the back, who poked Gilbert with her pencil. "When you're ready," Mrs. M said, "then add one more verse. Let it begin with the words 'Someday I . . .' "—and she got up from her desk to write that on the chalkboard. "Put that down and see what comes with it." This was an addition of her own to Koch's exercise.

Perhaps I should have written a poem along with them, but the moment I began it came to me how much this could reveal about a person—and besides, I was only there to take notes for a report to the doctoral seminar, where a scholarly critique would be expected. A critique supported by citations from the literature, of course—and this exercise suggested one from the anthropologist Jules Henry. He points out that when middle-class people think of their individual selves they say in effect, I *used to be* that way; here is the way I *am now,* and I hope I *will change* for the better. They think of themselves as changing, developing—having before them the possibility of someday achieving greater personal power—and from this view of the self as changing derives their conception of time as a progression.

But where there is little hope of personal growth and each day is much like another, this conception of time cannot develop. In some languages the word for tomorrow also means today. "No one spoke about the future at all," George Packer says of the Ewé, and what awed him most about them was "their feat of doing the same thing, or nothing, day after day, without the hope of anything ever changing." The name of the village in which he lived, Lalaviadé, means Wait a Little More. "It's because we don't care about time that we Africans are underdeveloped," an official told him. But where there is little hope for the future there is little concern for time, and one lives then within an endless present.

This is true of many young people, Henry suggests, who come into the schools from depressed neighborhoods and housing projects. Lacking the hope of good things to come, they have no reason for organizing their time and so their behavior often seems capricious, irregular, unordered. They have become survival selves in flight from death, finding some momentary satisfaction in those intense sensations which give one the feeling of being really alive. But when individuals have the hope of change, then the temporal dimensions of the self develop as they organize their behavior for achievement, striving to move from what *used* to be toward what *will* be. Which suggests that the variant behaviors we observe in schools may spring in part from the different time worlds in which people live.

But none of this could have been known to Mrs. M. I mean, she hadn't read Jules Henry or Martin Heidegger on time. She had read the poets and could come up with an appropriate quote from Robert Frost, say, or Shakespeare, but otherwise she wasn't well-read or intellectual. And yet, here she was using an exercise that carried out Henry's thought and virtually in his own words. An exercise borrowed from a poet, true, but extended from past and present to include the future, as though she and the poet both were in sympathetic vibration with young people, their intuitions attuned to the emotions simmering silently in the room. Or sometimes not so silently.

"Well, what shall we do with these?" Mrs. M asked, looking up from her desk. "This could be interesting."

"Do we gotta read 'em out loud?" Letty asked.

"I'm not going to read mine out loud. If you've got something really personal you can just put it away—but we're all friends here, so let's see what we've got. Trade with someone nearby. This could be interesting," and she handed her own paper over the desk to Dan. Gilbert, I noticed, slid his into a notebook and reaching across the aisle pulled Letty's poem from her desk. As he held it up before his face, reading, Letty reached over stealthily and took his notebook. "Hey!" he said, suddenly aware of what she was doing: "Gimme that!" And standing up he grabbed for it as she leaned away holding it just out of reach and shrieking "What you hidin here, huh? What you hidin?" He was lying across her now, snatching for the notebook. "They at it again!" Sheree said, disgusted, but the others were enjoying this, calling out "Go for it, brother!" and "You got'im, sister!"

Mrs. M watched all this impassively from her desk, and then as Gilbert managed to retrieve his notebook she got up and turned to the chalkboard. "What's in there, bro?" Dan called out from the front, trying to keep the excitement going. "None yo damn business!" What *was* he hiding?

"Let's look at those last lines," Mrs. M said, "and find out what we're hoping for. You have someone's paper there, my friend," she was looking at Gilbert, "so start us off. Someday I . . . ?"

He picked up Letty's paper. "It say 'Someday I will die.'"

"Oh, that's heavy, that's serious! Does anyone else have one like that?" I hardly expected to hear about death from these lively youngsters, and yet there were five more references to it, so Mrs. M wrote "Someday I will die" on the chalkboard, saying "So here is one of our themes, one of the thoughts we have on my minds. We have serious people here, we have serious thoughts, we have"—she was murmuring now into the quiet room—"other themes. Who will give us one?"

Sheree said "How bout this one: 'Someday I will take my love / and build with her something sacred'? I like it."

"So do I. Has anyone else mentioned love?" And we heard a few more lines that spoke of love, happy or disappointed, of marriage, and in one case of an urgent need for sex—which provoked an outburst of approving laughter. "Yeah, man!" someone called out. As Gilbert reached over and poked Letty in the ribs she slapped his hand away saying loudly "Keep *offa* me!" and there was more laughing. "Tell'im, sister!" I thought the class was much too restless, too noisy, but Mrs. M only turned back to the board and wrote Take My Love, underlining the last word.

"Alright—what other themes do we have?" she asked. There were two, each spoken of more times than either love or death: success ("Someday I will have a good job"; "Someday I'll be rich") and identity ("Someday I will find myself"; "Someday I will put away the mask and / find a place where people will accept me as I am / without a single question asked"). And then there were a few last lines spoken alone, expressing some sad yearning thought ("I used to live / Now I don't / Someday I'll be back / someday") or still lingering pain ("Someday I will dig a deep hole / and bury his green eyes there / secretly"—although this, some were sure, must be love; "No, I hate'im!" the writer announced).

"So we are concerned with love, death, success, and identity," Mrs. M said, "and these are the great themes of life. Which one of them should we go into, which one of them should we work with?"

"Sexcess," Dan said.

"What's that you said? Excess?"

"*Sex*-cess!"

"O-oh. Alright, success in love has been proposed—what do the rest of you say? Do you—" but the bell rang abruptly, ending the period, and as if by conditioned reflex the youngsters got up at once, noisily, moving toward the door in a babble of talk. As Gilbert passed by after Letty, Mrs. M reached out to touch his shoulder and he stopped there by her desk reluctantly, with a what's-the-problem-now look. He was the most disruptive one. But then as she spoke he opened his notebook and pulling out a sheet of paper gave it to her. She glanced at it, reading quickly, then as he turned away I heard her say "I like you, my serious friend." "Thanks," and he went on, leaving the paper there. And of course I asked to see it.

> I used to many things that roused my family sadness
> Now I am doing things that bring them happiness
> I used to stay out many times
> Now I stay in so I commit no crimes
> I used to think that I was really bad
> Now I believe the things I did were sad
> Someday I will return home to let everyone know
>   I've really changed.

It surprised me that he would in a few moments put down such things about himself there on a page that could slip from his hands and be revealed. "How did you know they would do this?" I asked. "It's such a restless crowd, I never thought they would be that serious about writing a few lines."

"Well, there are all these things that worry them, and they sit in school all day holding it all back, waiting. But I can use those worries, we can get something good out of them."

"But how did you know you would get something useful doing this? I mean something you can go on with, like finding those themes?"

"Oh, we take our chances." Another crowd of youngsters was pushing into the room and in a moment she would begin her next class. "We'll talk later," she said, and moved toward the doorway to greet each new arrival as I went out. The corridor was noisy with the press of youngsters streaming along in both directions like the crowds on a city street hurrying to be on time as later they would be hurrying home. The bell rang again and a few stragglers slipped by closing doors or lingered briefly for a goodbye look, leaving the locker-lined corridors to official traffic. What would she do next in that class, I wondered, now that she had found those themes? Or had they been dropped at the sound of the bell? "Someday I'll be back / someday"— the words drifted into my mind like the refrain of a song.

When she came to the table for lunch and glanced at my notebook, open and ready for answers to my questions, her demeanor was suddenly brusque and she set her tray down sharply. "I suppose," she said, "that what you're looking for are the good things that happen, the so-called good lessons. Well, just remember to report that most of my classes are very routine. In fact, if you'll come to that class again Monday you'll see a very routine lesson. One of our more usual days."

What had provoked this? "But those poems, those themes— what are you going to do with them?"

"Nothing! Not on Monday. Monday we get out the reading workbooks. We're going to have a reading lesson!"

She looked down at her plate, fork in hand as if considering whether to attack the carrots or the macaroni. The reading supervisor, she said, had just stopped her in the corridor and announced a visit. "So now we'll have to go through the motions to please her. I've been putting it off for weeks, but Dr. Fox told me he needs the quarterly report, so for his sake I'm letting her in." That explained it, and she speared a carrot. "Be sure to get this into your paper—the routine time we put in, the daily monotony of it all." Here was a side of her I hadn't seen, the reverse of her usual optimism, so I thought it best to keep quiet as she talked on, indignantly loquacious. "You hardly get some-thing good started before the bell rings or the guidance depart-ment sends in a messenger or there's an announcement over the intercom, breaking the rhythm. 'How sour sweet music is / when time is broke and no proportion kept.' You know those lines, of course." I looked at her blankly. "*Richard II.* What *do* they have you reading at the university?"

"Oh, very important things. How to teach writing—we read about that. And reading—what to do with a story or poem. And some criticism and theory, of course. Structuralism is very big right now."

"Well, I suggest you read a novel. Any novel—or Shakespeare even. Something rhythmical that doesn't clunk along." She turned her attention to the carrots and we ate in silence, until finally after the macaroni I thought it safe to say something.

"I suppose you know that what you're doing with poetry writing is not favored by our advanced thinkers"—and even as the words were coming out of my mouth I knew this was a mistake but I couldn't stop and went blundering on, saying "I mean, giving them sentence starters and forms to fill in, when every word should come from them, from their free expression, you know. Not be imposed. You know what I mean." I was only trying to be supportive in a sort of ironical way.

"Do I care what they think?" she asked, dropping the flat of her hand down onto the table top in exasperation, her fork clattering against the formica. "When I give my young people one of those forms I'm asking them to take a certain point of view, to assume a particular stance toward their experience. It's like acting out a role in a play, only *they're* writing the part, acting out their own lives." She hesitated. "I suppose I could say more about this if I thought about it but I'll leave that to your advanced thinkers."

She had been speaking loudly enough to attract the attention of other teachers at nearby tables, and noticing this she lapsed into silence. I thought of her as she had been earlier that day in her classroom, standing before the chalkboard and murmuring encouragement. "Well, time to go!" she said, glancing up at the clock. "We live in a time-hungry world"—and gathering up her books from the table she left the lunchroom for her next class, and I for the university to meet with the advanced thinkers.

What she was trying to do, it seemed to me, was live in a different time world than the ticktock world of the school, but how could she ever succeed at that? She wanted to introduce into the classroom an element of contingency, allowing activities to develop according to the chance thoughts that came with the interactions there and so make room for the unexpected. She wanted her young people to live with her (she might say if she thought about it) in narrative time rather than in expository time when learning is fragmented into morsels given one after another. She wanted them to come away with something to talk about, with a story to tell, rather than with facts to repeat. But the fact is that we must all learn to live in a ticktock world, however much we might wish it otherwise, and the school is organized for that purpose.

The class began Monday with Mrs. M at the door handing out workbooks to the youngsters as they came in, speaking quietly to each. The reading supervisor had taken Gilbert's seat in a back corner and he stood over her silently demanding his place, but she continued making an entry on her notepad so he sat down in Letty's place. "Hey, you got my seat, boy!" she

said, pushing against him with a hip, but then settling into a
neighboring seat. Two other students contested for the next seat
along the file, one displacing the other and creating a rush for
seats by those who usually sat in the back, until by a game of
unmusical chairs everyone found a place, the usual absentees
having left room enough. The conversational hubbub moderated
somewhat as Mrs. M closed the door. "Today is our reading
day, of course," she said, speaking as if it were a regular
occurrence, "so let's turn to page 31. You have twenty minutes
for this page, and when the time is up we'll review your answers
to the questions."

I expected to hear some vocal objection, at least, if not a
protest, but the youngsters dutifully opened their workbooks
and began reading, the increasing silence silencing the talkers.
So they'll go along with her and play the game, I thought.
They're used to the arbitrariness of teachers, who are so concerned about something one day and something else the next.
But then as they continued to read on quietly the thought came
to me that perhaps they like doing these routine exercises,
finding in them rest and safety. They were unusually peaceful.

Each double-columned page of the workbook gave four
paragraphs followed by multiple-choice questions testing a reader's comprehension. To begin a page was to enter a world of
right or wrong, where the answers to every question had been
predetermined and complete certainty was possible in the end.
There is considerable comfort, perhaps, in resigning oneself to
the authority of a workbook. But I was bored, and reaching
across the aisle I signed to a nearby youngster, wanting to borrow
his notebook. He nodded, so I picked it up from the floor and
leafed through, looking for the poem. He had given it a title,
writing several words in an upper corner and crossing out each
in turn until one remained that satisfied him.

Progress

I used to crawl
Now I walk.
I used to walk
Now I run.
I used to run

Now I sit here
  gazing out the window.
Someday I will leave
  and this will have no meaning.

That was the final version, after he had crossed out his first try for a last line and written in a shorter version of the same thought. As a piece of work dashed off on demand in a few minutes, this seemed to me unusually good—expressive and ironic. He had penciled his name in one corner of the paper, and I glanced over expecting to see him sitting there bored, staring out the window, but he seemed engrossed in the workbook. Steve—a thin, little guy. Looking at him, who would know he had such thoughts? And perhaps they surprised him as well, once they were on paper speaking back to him. The form of this poem had given him a channel through which could flow the force of his feeling intellect and by it he could know himself. What had the others done with this, I wondered?

Unobtrusively, quietly, I got up and went along the aisle asking to look at notebooks, to borrow a poem—until sent back to my seat by a stern look from the reading supervisor. But the poems I did get were interesting, most of them having at least one expressive line—a regret or hope or fear—the concerns or yearnings of the young. I began copying a poem of cynical wisdom into my notebook: "I use to think I would save the world an help everybody / Now I know people wont change an some are hopeless"—when someone said loudly "It bout the beer cans!"

"I don' get it," she went on—a girl sitting in the middle of the room who had raised her hand, apparently, and was now responding to a quizzical look from Mrs. M. "See, it say in the paragraph he see these beer cans on the mountain, but he jes making that up, he like exaggeratin, right? But there no answer for that, it like you gotta agree with it."

"That's paragraph 4 this careful reader is talking about. Has everyone read it? What do you say—are the beer cans there or not?"

Paragraph 4 described the view from a remote mountain top which the writer had reached after an arduous climb, leaving behind the noise and the detritus of the city. ("Detritus is: (a) traffic; (b) rubble; (c) lights; (d) garbage.") But at his feet among the rocks were two old beer cans. "Yeah," a boy said, "I'd take my beer." "Climbin a mountain?" Cherelle demanded scornfully. "Get real! Beer cans is heavy." And besides, she'd seen places like that on television and they were beautiful and clean.

"But there's trash *everywhere*," someone told her. "That's the point. Don't believe everything you see on TV."

"I got the point!" Cherelle said. "He like exageratin!" She was getting angry.

During all this the reading supervisor looked on, struggling against an impulse to intervene, nearly rising once from her seat then settling back, raising her hand momentarily as if asking for attention then pulling it down. "Alright," Mrs. M said, breaking through the side conversations that had begun around the room, "let's move on. Most of us don't seem to agree with you on that, but—"

"So you sayin I'm wrong!" Cherelle said.

"Well, let's say you haven't convinced us, okay? But let's go over our answers to all these questions and see if we can agree." It was obvious this crowd was not going to settle back down to silent reading. She picked up the answer sheet and read out the first five answers as the youngsters checked their choices—and immediately loud objections were raised against one of the answers, hardly anyone having chosen correctly. They knew they were right, they had reasons, and the conversations began again. "Alright," Mrs. M told them, "I'll correct the answer sheet." The reading supervisor sat back, resigned, waiting for her moment to come. Outside the day had darkened, making the fluorescents in the room seem even brighter.

As the bell sounded and the youngsters rose to go out, dropping their workbooks onto the teacher's desk and hurrying by, the reading supervisor moved quickly among them to the front of the room where Mrs. M waited for her. Standing a tactful distance away I could hear only a few words above the noise, although the supervisor had turned as if to include me in her audience. "But they're not *supposed* to discuss the paragraph," she was saying. "They have to make their own individual choices! And they have only a few minutes to do it in." Mrs.

M murmured something, looking quizzical, and the supervisor said "Yes!—they have to learn why an answer is wrong. We don't vote on it. They must learn to think critically!" Mrs. M nodded agreeably, and in another moment the supervisor turned away and went out. Mrs. M rolled her eyes. "Wódahgo," she murmured. Overhead the sky rumbled again with an approaching storm and again, more loudly, she said "Wódahgo!" "What's that mean?" I asked. "It means stay above, stay away. Or in other words, get lost. I learned it from my Navajo grandmother. You're supposed to say it four times but I don't want to disrupt events completely. Words have power, as she would say." We were at the door by then, and she turned to greet the youngsters coming in, her manner pleasant but matter-of-fact as if to say, You have work to do. On her desk the workbooks were piled haphazardly.

By the time we met for lunch her usual good humor had returned and with an almost insouciant air she put her tray down on the table. "I just could not do that again with the next class," she said. "I've asked her to come next week and show me how it's done."

"Will she do it?"

"Not if she's smart. The idea appealed to her, but when she thinks about standing before that crowd she may think again. Unless she really wants to show me a thing or two." We removed our dishes from the trays—carrots again, and pasta shells in tomato sauce. "I hope you're going to write up that reading lesson," she continued. "Be sure to report the very ordinary, routine food I served today." Picking up a fork she poked into the pasta.

"If it weren't for that, the reading lesson I mean, what would you have done with them today? Go on where you left off?"

"There's no way to recapture that moment now. When they come back after the bell has separated us, and then the workbook, they'll have forgotten what we were talking about so I'll just have to go on. We found a theme to work with and I'll take my cue from that, even though we haven't talked about it enough. I'll need a good love story—and we'll read it right there, all of us together."

"But what about those poems? Aren't you going to do something with them?"

"Oh those aren't poems, you know. The one you showed me— Steve's—that was nearly a poem because he'd worked on it some, shaped it, gave it a title. An ironic title too. But he needs a little more time with it. It takes time to draw away from the others long enough to create a quiet space filled with thought—and forty-five minutes isn't enough. We should have twice the time and then I could really get something going! Or so I like to think. It's so easy to find reasons why good things don't happen. Just remember what I told you when you write that report: be sure to tell how ordinary and routine most of my lessons are."

"Oh, that report—I'm thinking of writing it as a narrative, only I'm not sure that's going to be acceptable. You see, the expository parts where you explain things tend to drop out when you're writing narrative, they're not interesting. And I've got all these little stories, anecdotes, and I'd like to find a theme that would pull them together." I was warming to the subject, I'd been thinking about this, and she was listening so I went on. "Stories are interesting because they have conflict, drama— and you're always stirring people up, you're a troublemaker! You want to live here in narrative time rather than simply mark time as you were doing this morning."

"I'll tell you what I want here—I want *hoeshk!* But that's just between us." It would have to be, I thought, not knowing what she meant. "Hoesh?—is that what you said? What's that?"

But she was already gathering up her books. "No time to explain now, when duty calls. If we're going to talk about hoeshk we'll need a quiet place and plenty of time. A drink might help too." And getting up from the table she hurried away as the bell rang for the end of the period, leaving me there alone with the trays and empty plates.

And a few notes I'd managed to get down as we talked. She had been cheerful and self-assured as usual, speaking confidently and surprising me occasionally with an unexpected turn of thought. And now a thought she had turned from rather quickly, even anxiously, drew my attention: "It's so easy to find reasons why good things don't happen"—as if in complaining about the shortness of time she had only been finding an excuse for not doing better work with her youngsters. But how could she do any better with thirty or more young people five times a day, five days a week? Her sense of guilt, if that's what it was, seemed to me unwarranted. But so often we are put into these impossible situations and then made to feel guilty when good things don't happen. Whenever some activity well begun was abruptly terminated by the clock before finding its own completion she must have felt ineffectual. She would be reminded then of the easy efficiency of other classrooms, their precise completions contrasting with the half-finished experience in hers. But there was nothing to be done about this except go on.

"We do the best we can in the time we have," I said later that week, thinking to offer some consolation when once again the bell had broken the rhythm of her class. "There's only so much time in a day and they do have to go on to another subject."

"Why?" she asked. "Why not meet for twice the time but not so often? As it is we tell youngsters not to get too involved with this work—don't get interested because in a few minutes you'll be moving on to another room and another subject. They're here for training in time-discipline, that's our real aim."

"But that's necessary, isn't it? Most of these kids are going on to jobs where they'll have to live by the clock and leave all their personal concerns behind. They have to learn how to do that—that's life."

"Not the life I want to live! Let someone else do that training—and this whole school is devoted to it. Surely there ought to be some time in the day when we can live another way. But there's no respect here for hoeshk, no interest in that at all."

"How can there be when we don't know what it is?"

"That's the problem!" She nodded affirmatively and smiled. I wondered if she were putting me on, if she had invented this word as a way of referring to her own time-relaxed practice, to her ideal of the teaching life. If so, she might have invented a more euphonious term for it, rather than this odd word with a velar snap at the end: hoeshk. "What is it?" I asked again, but again the time was not propitious.

And I had my paper to prepare for the seminar. By now it

seemed that I should find a way to contrast institutional time with the narrative time in which Mrs. M lived—the time of clock-ordered sequences as against the use of past, present, and future in the unpredictable expression of memory, feeling, and expectation. But the danger of that would lie in moralizing time, in defining the routine schedule as unnatural, less humane. After all, some school subjects have their own natural logic and seem to dictate their schedule of development without reference to memories or feelings or hopes. And a secure future for most people depends on their learning to live in a clock-governed world. Or can a school find ways to recognize a multiplicity of times?

When I came to observe again, Dan was at the chalkboard writing some lines under the day's objective—the same objective that was always there: To understand that language makes thought possible.

"As you know," Mrs. M was saying, "our poet is in charge today. And I think he has a new poem for us."

"A song," Dan said. "One of my songs."

"Sing it!" Letty called out.

"If my backup was here I would, but you can help. See, let me explain this. We don't perform for an audience. It's not like you go to a concert hall and you sit there and you listen. We perform *with* the audience. See, they make the moves, they make the sound—that's what music is all about today. So I want you to do it with me. It's called "No Escape," and I'll do the verse and you come in on the chorus." He waited a moment. "Now come on, be serious. We'll do this once for practice, and then we'll all perform. Are you ready? Okay—" and moving in the rhythm he began declaiming the song:

> Stop to listen, be cautious
> steady yourself with care
> the things you find inside
> may not really be there.
>
> Suicide a one-way ride
> could save me from this cell
> catch the tide or live to hide
> in this gleaming hell.

"Now join me on the chorus, everybody—let's go":

Chosen by machine
never a mistake
supremacy wins
gives no break
real freedom goes
to those who take
that's life's injustice
no escape.

"Hey, that's okay. Now let's really get into it, I can't do this by myself. I want you and you and you—all you five sitting right there—you say my lines along with me. Not too loud, just a normal tone. And don't try to be smooth together, just these different voices stumblin around for backup. And then everybody come in strong on the chorus. You got it? Are you with me? Okay, now let's do it!" And this time he shouted out the lines against a background of other voices with all the confidence of a practiced performer, marking the rhythm with gestures, an arm-waving body-twisting rocker, though somewhat restrained here. The performance ended with a burst of applause that I was sure could be heard down the corridor.

What would others think of this, I wondered—this rhythmical play with suicide? Suppose some anxious parents were to hear of it, the gleeful even jubilant expression of those dark aspects of the adolescent soul they would rather believe will fade away of themselves in time if only ignored. They could give this teacher some real trouble and feel so good about it, showing their concern for the children.

"I don' get it," Letty said. "What you mean bout things inside not really there?"

"I don't know," Dan said. "What's it mean to you?"

"Well, like if I feelin sad inside I know it, it *be* there. It really be there. So how you say no?"

"It's like maybe you feel sad," Sheree said, "but you got no good reason. Is that it?"

Or like maybe, I thought later, you feel a sense of emptiness, as though giving up the effort to be as others would have you has uncovered no self of your own. Suicide has been called the disease of hope, when vision is blocked, the future lost, and one is unable to see beyond Saturday night. For how many young people does time stand still, an endless present broken mechanically during the day by a series of bells providing a semblance of movement, as though decisive endings and new beginnings are really possible, everyday events? In a world themed with uncertainty, anxiety, and violence they may no longer believe the promise made to them that sitting in school-rooms hour after hour will bring satisfaction and success some fine day. Suicide becomes a form of social criticism—or is that reading too much into a schoolboy's song?

"These songs you've given us," Mrs. M said, "they all seem sad or angry or violent. Is that a convention? I mean, are they all doing it or is this something you're really feeling yourself?"

"Oh they're all doin it, the bands I dig like Bio Hazard and Mucky Pup and Killing Time, and they *mean* it! But the bands that go big time, go commercial you know, some of them're doin it too but with them it's just pretending." And before anything more could be said the fire bell clanged.

"Two by two!" Mrs. M called out, sorting the youngsters crowded at the door into pairs as they passed by. We all walked along the corridor, waited for the class in the next room to stream out ahead of us, Letty and Gilbert holding hands, I noticed, and then down the stairs and out into the parking lot. In one corner a lone tree was already showing green buds, and as the youngsters passed out of the building into bright spring they broke away from their ordered lines and mixed about, seeking each other, calling out. Mrs. M stood against the wire fence, waiting. "When are you going to tell me about hoeshk?" I asked. "Did I say it right?"

"It needs a little more snap at the end, but you're close. That's something we can talk about in spring, so the season is right, but it must be spoken of after dusk and where the atmosphere is encouraging."

"Leave it to me, I know just the place."

So early one evening we met in a restaurant off Eighth Avenue, sitting for a dinner of genuine Italian pasta served over a checkered cloth while piano notes drifted to us across the room. As I poured the second glass of wine, she said "This is very pleasant. And music is appropriate too, because in the Navajo way we should make music of our lives."

"That sounds good," I said while preparing myself for a disappointment. There's enough mysticism available without borrowing more from the noble savage. "But how do we live musically today?"

"Well, we can make songs for one thing, or learn songs at least. Among the Navajo a person who has no songs is considered poor. My grandmother died murmuring one of hers. You see, the idea is to live so that you are in harmony with your people and with the world that has been given to us—and that is hoeshk. It's the word for beauty—not beauty as only something to appreciate but as a way to live."

"That sounds good," I said again, not wishing to disturb our evening with a doubt.

"But?" she asked, looking at me as though amused. "Not practical enough for you, I suppose. Well, the Navajo are very practical. They've had to make their way through this life against aggressive enemies in a desolate land, and dreaming feeds no one. But even so, the making of beauty is part of their lives. A Navajo will tell you to walk in beauty, speak in beauty, act in beauty—everything you do is to be completed in beauty. It's the *way* you act that's important, you see, not some end result. After the sand painting has been made it's destroyed. The virtue is in the doing! So beauty has to be continually renewed in your life if you are going to live well." She hesitated. "Do you see that? There's no word in English for this, no word that sums up the unity of experience as hoeshk does—that brings art and the moral life together."

"It reminds me of Keats saying that beauty is truth, truth beauty. And then there's Wittgenstein's remark that ethics and aesthetics are one. He must have had something like hoeshk in mind, but of course he was something of a mystic. And a poor teacher too, by the way. He went back years later to find his students and apologize to them."

Nodding thoughtfully she picked up her wine glass, and in that quiet moment I felt uneasy, as though I'd made some sort of blunder, babbling along. To break the uncomfortable silence I said "What more can you tell me about this?"

"Well, I think it would please your rational mind to know that the Navajo consider thought to be masculine. And language, by the way, is feminine." She smiled. And I smiled back uneasily, feeling the light sting of a barb concealed in those remarks without being able to find it at the moment. But after all, there's nothing wrong with being rational.

Only later did I begin to see the implications in what she was saying and understand better what she wanted to make of the brief time given her each day with a group of youngsters. Her concern was not with carefully plotted beginnings and endings for her lessons but with middle moments, which surrender first and last things to concentrate on expressions of creative power. These moments she would craft with care, expecting them to become suffused with the cultural essence of the community there within the room—and the youngsters would leave carrying with them a memory of their time together, a moment of poetic beauty made as a consequence of their having lived and worked in this community of their fellows. And this experience fading away into the past might become one of those "spots of time" that Wordsworth spoke of, which still retains "A vivifying virtue, whence . . . our minds / Are nourished and invisibly repaired."

As we left the restaurant and came out into the darkness of a warm spring evening I stepped to the curb, looking for a taxi. The traffic lights along the avenue were turning sequentially red to green, and with the green a taxi at the corner jerked into motion and swerved over to us. "Good night," she said, hesitating at the open door, "and may you walk with hoeshk. I haven't been able to say that to anyone for a long time."

Chapter 5

The Concealments of Style

Having a style means having developed the flaws in your character to the point where they bring you a satisfying return. To the point, that is, where you are regarded well by others or even admired for the very characteristics they would condemn in you if only they recognized them for what they really are. But thanks to an artful self-presentation they do not. A presentation that can never be spontaneous, of course, but is like all art the result of conscious effort and unremitting practice.

Spontaneity, after all, is a quality much overrated. To be spontaneous is to be natural or genuine, and this is commonly thought a good thing even though first impulses are rarely generous and not to be trusted. Spontaneity in lovemaking, for example, can hardly be recommended. There are now guidebooks readily available on the art of making love, and many people have benefited from their instruction since a thoughtful lover is far more satisfying than all those who are simply trying to express themselves. To be spontaneous is to express your own need in the most obvious way, and that is the opposite of having style. But to create from the drossy defects of your character a presentation of self that wins the favorable regard of others, or at least their indulgence, is a feat comparable to turning straw into gold. It requires consciously applied effort and a touch of magic as well.

Although quite unstylish in her everyday appearance, Mrs. Martinez had attained an individuality of style and made herself present in the world. Certainly in the school world that was her field of action, where she was thought an interesting character by some, while others considered her unserious, even frivolous.

Changes in program, in theory and practice, all passed her by with the years as she went an independent course, creating a zone in which tongues were loosened and style might have a beginning.

She came along the corridor smiling, carrying a small book in one hand. "At last I have it!" she told me, holding the book up so I could read the cover. "The answer to all our problems." It was *The Elements of Style*, by Strunk and White. "That's an old favorite," I said, "but usually they give it to college freshmen."

"Well, our department head gave it to me." We went into her classroom to wait for the third-period seniors. Up on the wall over the chalkboard a large colored print of a tiger moving stealthily through long grass was taped by the corners, and we sat down at the teacher's desk under it, Mrs. M saying "These seniors need more style, you see, and so we're all looking for the book that will show them the way."

"I suppose when you find it you can stack the copies over there under the window with the grammar books and forget it."

"Of course. And this is just another grammar book, really, with rules to follow and errors to avoid. Here's one— Rule 17: 'Omit needless words.' Now isn't that helpful? But my problem here is to get more words, not fewer. I'm lucky to get a paragraph or two from most of these people."

"That book is so outmoded I'm surprised anyone would recommend it. We don't talk about style nowadays, you know, we talk about voice. You're supposed to help young people find their individual ways of expression, so they will write in their own natural voices, honestly. Or something like that."

"Well, that sounds good but that's a crock—if I may say so in my own natural voice. Of course I don't go around talking this way. I could develop a confrontational style but it would do me no good, people would hate me. So I just keep quiet while the latest fashion in pedagogy goes by. Now this one— finding your own natural voice. Oh yes. But of course a voice isn't something you find, it's something you develop, you make. We can get all these natural, sincere outpourings from young people, but if anything is going to come of them they have to be worked over and formed—presented. But only a few will go to all that trouble."

"And the others?"

"If they'll write a few coherent paragraphs I'll be satisfied. Plain, impersonal prose—that's what we live with every day, that's what we need. So that's all I'm asking for from these youngsters, just a little clear thinking in a few plain words."

But that's not true, I thought, because she's always looking for the self-expressive. Every time I thought I had her understood she would say something like this and confuse me. There was something perverse about the woman. "So how do we get this clear thinking in a few plain words?"

"By writing poems, of course," she said, and I was sure that in spite of her carefully serious expression she was laughing.

"But that can't be the whole story because—" and then a bell vibrated outside in the corridor, announcing the end of the period, and in a moment youngsters exuberant between classes were crowding noisily into the room. I got up to take a seat in the back, intending to watch very carefully.

The last time I'd been here was more than ten years ago, and if this was not the same room at least the fluorescent lighting and yellow walls and vinyl-tiled floor were familiar. The young-sters were different, with many fewer white faces among them. This group coming in was an interesting one, she told me when I asked to visit a class, one that would give me what I needed, she thought. But so far these youngsters had spent the previous three periods reading and writing and talking among themselves, either here or in the library. I wondered if any of the classes with Mrs. M would be as I remembered. That's what I needed.

Malcolm came slouching in almost late, wearing a back baseball cap with a large white **X** on it, and his jeans pulled down to display an inch or two of underwear—a jailhouse style, copied from prisoners who were not allowed to wear belts. A tough look. "You tol us liberry agin," he was saying truculently, lounging along, jeans bagging at the seat, "but nobody down there . . ." and Mrs. M turned to join him, doing his loose walk and saying in rhythm with him "Hey man, what you mean, liberry? We all comin right on here, jes like . . ." until he turned his head away to smile and sat down, sliding his long legs out into the aisle, displaying a new pair of high-top sneakers, laces hanging untied. "Nice tops," Mrs. M said. Yeah, he nodded, pleased. It had been a five-second duet, hardly noticed by the others busy talking.

"Alright," Mrs. M said, turning to the class, "today we will hear—" but then a boy sneezed loudly, theatrically, then again. The laughter he'd started, and the comments, faded as she turned to him. "Do you really need attention that much?" she asked sympathetically. "Now first today we will hear from a researcher who will tell you something she's found out about us. So with her permission I now introduce Miss Shakena Wells."

"Do I gotta read it?" she asked, getting up reluctantly, holding two or three sheets of paper. Her hair was arranged in elaborate box braids over her forehead and gathered at the back of her neck, while from each ear swung a large golden torus.

"It's your report," Mrs. M told her, easing into the chair behind Shakena's desk, "so do it however you like."

"Then I gonna sit down and tell you bout it." She went over to the teacher's desk, under the tiger print, and pulled out the chair. "Jes like Riley," Malcolm said loudly, referring to a social studies teacher who conducted all his classes from behind his desk.

"Well," Shakena began, "this bout hangin out. You member when my partner there comes in his arm all banged up? Some guy hit'im with a bat?" Nestor, leather-jacketed, rose slightly from his seat and nodded to right and left, acknowledging the calls and murmurs of sympathetic approval. "That give me the idea, so I say let's fine out bout hangin out. And he tol me do this. He say 'You do the outside an I do the inside,' so if this ain't no good it be his fault." She glanced down at her paper. "So I ax you all bout it, I get all this information—an I fine out you all hang out. Some a you doin nothin *but* hangin out! I fine out you all hangin roun Toys 'R' Us bout every night it warm, in the parkin lot."

"I see *you* there!" Malcolm called out.

"I doin my research! But you jes hangin roun."

"Oh yeah!" he said, leaning back in his seat, his legs stretched into the aisle on each side. He reached out his long arms and rested his hands on the shoulders of his neighbors, saying something to one then the other, and they laughed. Shakena was saying "You all hang out most every Fridy, Sa'dy night." As she went on Mrs. M got up, stepped back to Malcolm and leaning down whispered into his ear—a word, it seemed, and then she went back to her seat. "Now there's some people they got a boyfriend," Shakena was saying, "they got a girlfriend, so they not hangin out so much. You got a boyfriend, you not hangin out less you goin by seein if he be there. An he be there two, three nights, drinkin beer! I got the facts! Or he be hangin out roun the way, or he jes cruisin somewheres."

"So what's wrong with that?" demanded a boy sitting off to one side.

"I ain't sayin it's wrong, I sayin you doin it!"

"Yeah, what you doin tonight?"

"I ain't hangin out!" she said, speaking into the rising swell of sniggering laughter, "I got things to do. See"—and as she spoke Mrs M. rose again from her seat and turned back to a group of boys huddled in conversation, but one of them seeing her approach faced front again and the others took the hint—"you guys jes hangin out, but we busy, we goin to the store, we meetin our sister, we goin lookin for our guy, we—"

"Yeah, I *knew* it! You busy to-*night*!" And as her listeners laughed Shakena said "Now wait!"—trying to break through the noisy chatter—"Wait, I got a story." Mrs. M rose again, looking out over the room, and the restlessness subsided. "I got a story," Shakena said.

"See, Mondy night these outsiders come in, they come in to Toys 'R' Us, you know, an one of'em tries to run his car over one of the guys, so he starts fightin'im an the guy stabs'im in the back! So our guys take the bats an break his windshield an bottles were flyin an they chased'im out to the street an beat'im up with the bat. They left'im half dead right there by the street."

She had their attention. "See, all these guys gotta prove they the toughest, they the badest around."

"Yeah, I hear bout that," Malcolm said, turning to the boy behind him. "You there? You see it?" Everyone had to talk about this, the restless audience fragmenting into scattered groups, Shakena continuing with her eyewitness account to a few in front, Mrs. M too in a conversational huddle.

After a few minutes she got up, saying "I'd like to read Shakena's first paragraph to you." She reached for the paper. "It goes like this . . . " and as the talking faded she began reading:

> Once upon a time there was a toy store called Toys 'R' Us and all the little boys and girls used to go there with their mommies and daddies to buy toys. Then one night it so happened that some not so good boys and girls showed up at Toys 'R' Us but not to buy toys. They were hangin out. They came to drink, party and cause trouble.

She looked up. "That's very interesting. You had us all interested today. And I know your partner is ready with the rest of this report, so with his permission I now introduce Mr. Nestor James. Would you tell us the title of your paper?"

"It's 'Us and Them'" he said, standing up—a tall boy, strong, with the sides and back of his head shaved leaving a dome of lank black hair. "An I gotta tell you this so I can really do the scene." He leaned back casually against the side wall and put one foot up on the seat of his chair, at ease, enjoying the attention. "You know the Showplace down on the boulevard— you heard of it, right? So there's two bands scheduled to play this night. The first is Larceny. It's your standard thrash band that dabbles a little in punk, an they draw a big crowd cause they got a lot of friends an they're good. The other band was Mechanica. That's a basically heavy metal, poser type band. They had a big crowd there too. An so this entire setup was a mess right from the beginning, you gotta know it, cause when these two bands meet an play a show together there's gonna be a tremendous clash in the crowd!" He paused a moment, looking over this crowd tense with expectation—many of them the partisans of one music or another, and of the attitude or lifestyle expressed by it.

"See, my friends are all thrashers, hard core, or punk people. We like dancin, stage divin, and singin along in the mikes— we're basically physical people. But the metalheads, the guidos and the hair-spray broads, these people"—a mocking laugh broke out from one corner, and from a strong young man in a tight T-shirt an angry "Guidos?" but Nestor rushed on—"they just like to sit an watch the show or sing along from their seats.

What's even *worse* than the boring style these people got is their glam attitude, like they're better an more mature, but they're boring and drool like their music!" "NOT boring!" a voice called out, "Cool!" "Well, these people don't dance and they hate it! So it's plain to see there's gonna be some tension in this mixed up crowd."

Very plain. Again he paused, took a breath and spoke into the waiting silence, trying for a conciliatory tone but soon rushing along. "People are different, you know. So Larceny comes on an the place exploded with dancin an divin. All the Mechanica people went to the bar an billiard room to drink, playin pool an video games or watchin from a safe distance while we're having a great time! There was a few dark looks, you know, an some mumbled comments but it was cool so far. So Larceny finishes an then Mechanica sets up their equipment, an their friends pile onto the stage on grab chairs an sit down. An it was so *boring!* So me and my friend Ollie want to liven things up, so we begin to dance in a most mocking manner. Then Buster comes along. He's been loungin in the bar poundin down beers all night, an he was pretty hammered by now an he joins in. We continue our jolly for a while longer an then Ollie wants to dive. He climbs up on a table an flips off an we catch him. But Buster in his stupor can barely support himself an he staggers, he's dragging me along holdin Ollie above my head, and we stumble right into this crowd of guidos and hair-spray patients. They were okay but this one girl starts ragin—I mean just *ragin*, claiming that Buster kicked her—so her guy pushes him and oh, the winds of war swept into the Showplace! Buster ran at him in a drunken rage, his cousin Jay joins in an two more guidos start swingin so I push one over a chair an my friend P-Funk assaults the other one with a flurry of punches to the head an ribs. Then just when it's gettin into a real brawl the bouncers start breakin it up, an after ten minutes of spitting and threats it was all over. An all through this Mechanica kept on playin! So it just goes to show that you can*not* have two kinds of bands with conflicting views an music jammin in the same place. It's gonna bring pain an grief." He raised a fist and bent his arm to flex the biceps, then sat down.

This Nestor was a big, good-natured guy with a lot of rough

charm, so his readiness for violence, his pleasure in it, surprised me. The class had fragmented into conversational groups again, talking about music, but an especially noisy one where Malcolm was maintaining there wouldn't be so many fights if the girls didn't instigate them. Then the bell rang, and all these thrashers, rappers, punks, metalheads, and the unaffiliated crowded into the aisles still arguing, some of them, the superiority of one style over another.

In their appearance too they spoke a language of style, if only I had time to learn it. There was a conforming fashion—slacks and blouse for girls, jeans and hooded sweatshirt for boys—but in small variations on that fashion, or in a complete rejection of it, an attitude could be expressed, an individuality declared. The box braids, or long hair hanging down over a sweatshirt emblazoned with the name of a favorite band, the baseball cap worn backwards or a stud in one earlobe, pants pulled down on the hips—are ways of individually customizing the standard look and expressing to those who can read the signs a particular identity, on the principle that "To be is to be perceived." But of course these youngsters were speaking in this way to each other and I was only beginning to read the signs, let alone understand the individual concerns that might be concealed by the fashionable image. My purpose here, after all, was to understand what Mrs. M was doing, to get some idea of *her* style.

Not until lunchtime could we meet to talk, and then when we found a table to ourselves in the faculty cafeteria Riley came over and stood there, severe in a dark suit and necktie. "I want to ask you something," he told Mrs. M. "What are you doing in that third period class? They came into my room pushing and arguing and it took me awhile to settle them down, I had to get up and *demand* attention." He looked like a man nearly atremble with indignation but determined to maintain a sweet reasonableness. "You know Fridays are tough enough as it is."

"Well, we were having reports today, that's all."

"You were?"

"Yes. There was one on—let me think . . . the use of leisure time in the urban environment. And one on music as an expression of societal differences. What were you doing?"

He hesitated a moment, startled, then glanced at me but I

was keeping a straight face and hoping the effort didn't show. "Friday is quiz day," he said. "Weekly review and quiz, so they have to get serious. The war in Vietnam."

"That's important! It's been part of our lives, it's still affecting us. But I suppose they're more interested in Saturday night. You don't have an easy time with them."

"No, well . . ." and I thought he was going to sit down with us, but then he turned away saying "okay" and went back to his table.

Mrs. M picked up a spoon and began eating the canned fruit but I wanted to talk about this. "Now I see just how radical you are," I told her. "You're making divisions among the students, you're bringing out their differences. There's this surface uniformity they have—I mean some of them look a little different but they have a kind of public uniformity, they're getting along. But beneath the surface are all these antagonisms, all these social and class and ethnic differences—and you're bringing them out, you're stirring them up."

"Well, a little conflict will give us some drama. Or maybe even a laugh or two. We need that, you know."

She plays a very risky game, I thought. When you lecture a class or go by the book you're not taking any chances, the behaviors are determined in advance, there are few individual variations to deal with. I pulled over the dish of canned fruit. But with her way, you have all these attitudes and emotions to manage and who knows what's going to happen?

"And there ought to be a place," she continued, "where we can enjoy our differences now and then, don't you think? In a math class or science class they're irrelevant, they would just get in the way, but in my class we can find some advantage in our differences, we might get something good out of them. Or so I hope." She hesitated. "And how else am I going to keep up with youth culture? I don't want them to think I'm illiterate. I can do a mean Texas two-step but that doesn't count here, they're not interested in that."

It was true that I'd learned from Nestor about metalheads and divin and thrashers—and he told an entertaining story—but was that important? After all, it was just talk. "Why wouldn't they read their papers to us?" I asked. "That's the important thing, isn't it, what they write? But neither one of them would read to us, they'd rather talk."

"You take everything so seriously," she said.

"Yes, but why don't they read their papers to us? Then people would have to listen, they'd have to show some consideration— there wouldn't be interruptions all the time and we'd get the whole report. You wouldn't be getting up and going around telling people to be quiet. That's what you were doing, wasn't it?"

"Oh no, I was just whispering a word to them, to remind them. Respect, that's the word. They've heard it from me so often that usually I only have to stand up or look in their direction and they know what I mean. But today was a little more exciting than usual, so I had to say it now and then. Some lessons need a lot of repetition."

"But it just seems to me that if they would read a paper there'd be more serious consideration, more thoughtfulness. They have to learn how to listen, don't they?"

"Yes, and they *were* listening—they were being very responsive. You see, for many of these people being an audience means taking part in the performance, not sitting there passively. They get plenty of that training in their other classes. So I think that here we can be a congregation now and then. Do you agree?"

"Yes, but they get carried away so easily, they get so noisy! I still think it would be easier for them to read their reports to us, and safer—so why do they want to get up and make a speech?"

"Well, I give them a choice so if it were easier to read they'd do it, but obviously it's not. Nestor likes to get up and perform, so of course he doesn't want anything so formal as a written report separating him from the others, even though he writes very much like he talks. Writing makes for loneliness. And Shakena: remember when I read that paragraph of hers—how different her words sound from the page than when she's speaking? The written word sets her apart from the others— she's writing very well—and she doesn't want them to think she's setting herself up as better than they are. The other girls would put her back in her place soon enough. So she just tells it to us conversationally, being one of the crowd, almost like we're all hangin out somewhere."

I could have pointed out that Shakena's paper offered a very different experience than her talk about it. The paper had style, a point of view, and all the information she'd gathered—so why shouldn't the class have the experience of it? But before I could say more Riley was back, standing at our table again. "There's something else," he said. "Do you mind if I sit down?" and he pulled out the chair next to Mrs. M.

"We've been talking over there," he said, nodding toward the table he'd left, "and there's something else. It's these, well—paperclips, you know. We hear that's coming out of your fifth period class and it's making some problems, the natives are getting restless."

"I'm sorry about that," Mrs. M said. "What happened?"

"It happened right outside Harry's door." He nodded toward the other table again, indicating Harry sitting there. "Peter Redding goes up to this junior kid and he says 'Are you a clipper?' and he starts to hassle him. And Peter's a big guy."

What was this all about, I wondered. "Hassle him? How? I mean, what happened?"

"I told you. He said 'Are you a clipper?' and he grabs the paperclips off the kid's shirt, and then two more start mixing in. We hear it's all coming out of your fifth period class." He looked at Mrs. M, demanding an answer.

"Well, I'm sorry about that," she said. "We're doing an experiment but I'll cool them down. I told them to keep it to themselves."

Experiment? Riley sat there thoughtfully as if pulled between wanting to know and wanting to press his advantage. Then he said "You know, some people think it's just fooling around in your classes. I told them about those reports you're doing, one on leisure time—wasn't that it?—and that other one, but they think you're not serious at all."

Mrs. M looked at him thoughtfully, and then as she said "Well, perhaps I'm not too—" he went on speaking as though once begun there was no turning back the flow of long-felt dissatisfaction. "I mean you work, we all do, it's no picnic here, but there's just so much fooling around like with this paperclip thing. I can see what you're trying to do, get them interested with those reports and all that, but it's really social studies isn't it, or psychology or something. And what these kids really need is the discipline it takes to pay close attention to their language!" He settled back, evidently pleased with what he had just said because he nodded affirmatively and said again, "Close attention to their language."

Somewhat hesitantly, Mrs. M said "You mean they should learn their grammar."

"Yes! Their language is atrocious!" I could hardly believe it, that anyone still talked this way or actually believed that teaching formal grammar to the young would improve their language.

"I'm for that!" Mrs. M said. "It's important they learn to use their language well." He nodded along with her, satisfied to have scored the point. "You know," she said, "you started me thinking about something awhile ago. The Vietnam War. Some of these kids must know people who were there, they must have some interest in what happened."

"Oh no, that's something that happened a long time ago to somebody else. Ancient history—just something in a book. Harry there," he nodded toward his table, "he was an infantry captain in Vietnam but these kids don't know that. You think of all we've done—I mean, you too and all the rest of us—and they don't know and they don't care. They don't know us at all." The bell rang and around us people got up to leave. "It's like we're not really alive, you know." He had come to complain but stayed to share a sorrow.

As we left the lunchroom and walked along the crowded corridor, a girl wearing a necklace of linked paperclips nodded to us, touching it, and Mrs. M said "Oh yes" as she reached into a pocket, took out a paperclip with another dangling from it and attached it to the collar of her blouse. Then she hurried on to her next class, and I left for the university. If Riley hadn't taken up so much of our time we could have talked more, I'd be better prepared.

As the guest lecturer I was expected to be sensible about working with adolescents—about Techniques of Classroom Management, as the course guide had it. And what seemed important to me about this was not technique but style—and style is a matter of attitude, of being a particular kind of person. We can list teaching techniques, even put them into a book and sell it as a guide for beginners, but how do you describe style—that is, character—except by telling a story? And Mrs. M was a character, so I wanted to tell about her.

On Monday I was almost late for the class, arriving just as she took her place beneath the tiger print and speaking over the restless chatter said "Now if you will, our secretary is ready with his report on last week's work." Gregory stood up, with what looked like a horseshoe nail hanging from the lobe of one ear under a blue bandanna pulled tightly over the top of his head and knotted behind. He looked out over the crowd, a sheet of paper in one hand. As secretary he could use his report to single out individuals for such attention as he might wish to give them—and he was big enough to say whatever he liked.

"First thing last week I get elected secretary. Then our tall Italian friend comes in late again, so what else is new? An he had a wise saying for us. 'If you're born a cucumber don't try to be a tomato.' " This caused a reminiscent stir and someone said "Yeah, cucumber—is that what you are?" "At least I'm no fruit!" Gino said pointedly. "Who you callin a—" "Go on with your report," Mrs. M said.

"Then a beautiful lady read her questions to us bout hangin out and we wrote our answers. Then New Hightops asked us bout drinkin an druggin, an we wrote our answers. Tuesday we worked with our partners. Wednesday we wrote on our papers, an Mizzem—I mean, Our Glorious Leader—told us this really strange story about the spider woman. Thursday we were in the liberry, readin and writin. Then Friday was when Beautiful Lady gave us her report bout hangin out, an Thrasher gave his report bout the battle of the bands. An they were good! Now I'm suppose to say how I think the week was, an I think we did good. We got too much foolin around but we did good." He sat down.

"We thank you for that report," Mrs. M told him. "And now at this time I will accept nominations for the office of secretary. Do I hear a nomination?"

"Yeah—New Hightops," someone called out, and over his

protest Malcolm was elected. He was not pleased to have the extra work.

"As you know," Mrs. M continued, speaking over the murmur of talk, "we'll be working on our papers today. And two"—Malcolm was trying to get her attention, waving a hand and saying "Yo!"—"of our researchers have finished, so—" "Yo, MOMMA!" Malcolm called out. A hush fell over the crowd as Mrs. M turned her head, slowly bringing her gaze to rest on him. He was looking up at her with a little smirk, determined to brazen it out. "Yes, my son?" she asked.

"Why I gotta be secetary? I gotta be workin on my report, drinkin an druggin, I got too much."

"The people have chosen you, Mr. Secretary, because they know they can count on you. Right?" she asked the others and was answered with "Right!" "Right on!" "Yes, indeedy." "And remember, here's your chance to tell us a few things. You want to put us on the spot?—then go ahead. Just tell it like it is." She turned back to the class. "Now, two of our researchers have finished their papers, so they're available to hear what you've done so far. And I'll be working with you." She began walking slowly along the aisles, and gradually the talking subsided, the restless fidgeting. A young man slipped a paperback from his jacket as she passed by and began reading. "If I started shaving I'd have to do it every day," someone nearby was confiding quietly. Shakena pulled a chair over to another young woman and listened to her read a paper—about her mother, from what I could hear. Why that? I began jotting down my questions, to have them ready for our lunchtime meeting.

There was canned fruit to start with as usual, peaches this time, and as I opened my notebook between spoonfuls Mrs. M said "By the way, what do they say about me at the university?"

"Oh, you provoke a variety of reactions. There's a Brit, a Londoner, in the group and no matter what I say you're doing he says there's nothing new in that, they've been doing it in England for years. Someone else thinks you're eccentric but entertaining, and another one said you're not serious, you don't make the kids work hard enough. Her cooperating teacher is another Riley—he gives out those canned lessons and the weekly quiz."

"Oh I wouldn't be so quick to put Riley down," she said, looking at me sharply, making me feel for a moment like a schoolboy being reprimanded. "He has much to offer young people, he hasn't lived all his life in schoolrooms. I suppose you know why he sits down to teach." I didn't. "Because it pains him to stand for very long. And he's right, you see—these youngsters don't know anything about him and they're not interested. I think if he could see the humor in all this it would ease the pain, if it's not unkind to say so."

Not unkind perhaps, but no wonder some people thought she lacked seriousness. Yet by now I knew that was her way— to manage serious matters with a light touch, provoking others to speak from the heart while leaving unspoken her own concerns. It was her disposition toward others that made her skillful, not simply knowledge or long experience, for she was no more knowledgeable or experienced than Riley. The real difference between persons, Emerson said, is not in wisdom but in art—and I wanted to understand her art, to learn how she managed to charm forth the heartfelt imagery. "I was surprised when Riley told you he doesn't feel really alive here, as though he's only a ghost. He's very melancholy."

"He feels unrecognized. If the youngsters were interested in him enough to give him a name, that would help."

"But I'm surprised he would reveal himself to you like that, when he only wanted to complain. Why do people tell you these things?—that's what I want to know."

"They don't tell me nearly enough! I'm curious, that's all." No, there's more to it than that, I thought. And perhaps noticing my doubtful look she said "Well, I'll give you a clue. If you want people to show you what they are, then be a mirror. Don't try to express yourself, be a reflection." I must have been looking at her rather blankly, trying to think of myself as a reflection. "People never get tired of seeing themselves as they see themselves," she said patiently. "By the way, do you remember Ashton-Warner? Does anyone read her at the university now or is she forgotten already?" "She's a name," I said, "among all the other names." "Well, she was a nut of course, but my kind of nut. Everywhere she went she tried to draw out each person's key vocabulary, those few words with deep personal significance that are an index to the soul. And she could be very demanding about it, very insistent. Some people thought she was much too personal, too nosy, she made them feel uncomfortable. Well, I'm nosy too but I like to think I'm more subtle about it."

"Oh you are. And you can do it without the alcohol. But what I don't see is how you can do it in a classroom. I mean, reflection may work in a conversation, one on one, but these young people are so restless. And you sort of go along with the flow, you're always so calm whatever happens, so undemanding. How do you get them to do all these things, collect material and make reports?"

"I don't get many of them to do it. Shakena and Nestor and a few others, but the rest—I'm happy when they write a few paragraphs for us. And some of them won't even do that, so they bring a book to read. Sex and violence usually, but any reading they do is good for them." She hesitated, looking away for a moment. "You see, many of them are only biding their time here. And these classes are so large. I think the best we can do is help a few individuals."

I'd heard her say that before and it bothered me. Do we give up on most young people and find our satisfaction in the few who please us? "Like Shakena and Nestor?"

"Oh no, I just give them a place where they can use their talents. And the daily routine suits most of the others, they'll do alright. It's the difficult ones who interest me, the lost souls living under a curse—they're the ones who need us."

"So who are they? I mean, I don't see anyone you've been giving any special attention to." Perhaps I sounded a little petulant. I'd been observing that class very attentively and there couldn't be much I'd missed. But she was so devious in a way that it was difficult to know her well, and I thought she might be trying to provoke me even then.

Before she could answer, the implacable bell signaled the demands of the next period. Time had passed, the macaroni and cheese had been eaten, and now I had to leave with my notes still incomplete. So often she managed somehow in these conversations to ease away from my questions, leaving me with yet another puzzle instead of answers. Walking along the busy corridor toward the main entrance I passed two boys wearing paperclips linked into chains hanging from their clothes.

The next day I arrived early so as not to miss even the casual interactions before the start of class. The corridors of a school early in the morning, crowded with youngsters just come from bed and breakfast or still hungry, have a sound that is lacking later in the day after the routine has settled everyone, and Mrs. M was standing outside her room joining in the renewal of acquaintance. Then as the final bell sounded she closed the door and turned to her class—but the crowd was even more restless than usual, some of them still not in their seats, and Malcolm reached over to push Shakena's notebook from her desk, dropping it to the floor. Mrs. M stood beneath the tiger print, saying "If you will . . ." and waiting. "Some of you have stories for us today"—she was still speaking over their conversational exuberance—"so let me begin with a story, one that tells of two young people who went out into a dangerous world." And continuing to talk, moving slowly across the room and then along one side, reaching out a hand to touch the shoulder of a noisy one, she told a story that seemed to me entirely foreign to the urban life these youngsters knew, but as the words flowed on they were gathered in, watching her move slowly along the aisle and back.

> They say that twins are double trouble, but the twins I will tell you about were easy for their mother. Easy in the birthing and easy in the raising. But when they were old enough to understand the ways of men and women, they realized there was something strange about their coming into the world, for they had never seen their father, and their mother never spoke of him. When they asked her who he was she said, "You have no father." And when they asked her again she told them to stop bothering her, and that was all she would say. Finally they decided that when spring came they would go out into the world and search for their father.
>
> So when at last the fireweed bloomed and the pin grass was green, the Twins started out one morning in the cold air before dawn. They traveled rapidly, and by the time the sun was up they were far out on the barren lands, the

home of the snake and the scorpion. Some way off they saw a stream of smoke rising toward the sky, and wondering who was there they went closer. In the hard earth among the stones they found an opening large enough for a man to disappear into. Looking down they saw a room under the earth, and there by a cooking fire was an old woman, the Spider Woman.

"Welcome, my children," she said, calling to them. "Will you come down to visit me?" So the Twins climbed down the ladder that stood there in the opening, black with smoke.

"Where are you two going, walking together?" she asked them, and the Twins said, "Nowhere in particular." Three more times she asked them, but they told her nothing until she said, "Perhaps you are seeking your father."

"Yes!" the Twins answered. "If only we knew how to find the place where he lives."

"Oh," the woman said, "it's a long and dangerous path to the house of your father. Many monsters live along the way, and there are four places of danger you must pass through—the crushing rocks, the cutting reeds, the boiling sands, and the tall cactus that can tear you to pieces. But I will give you a charm to help you defeat your enemies and save your lives. Whenever danger threatens you must say, 'We go the beauty way.' And I will give you each a life-feather, for when you get to your father's house he may not be glad to see you. He may punish you for coming."

And Mrs. M went on, following the Twins through the four places of danger and then to their father's house, where his woman wrapped them in robes to hide them. I glanced around the room. If her aim had been to gentle them down, quiet them, she had achieved that for they were listening, sitting there isolated within their individual subjectivities, looking off into the distant world she was creating as she moved along the side of the room and back—except for one who had put his head down on his arm over the desk and closed his eyes. And two others in a far corner, more interested in each other than in any story. "And now they faced the greatest danger yet," she was saying,

for when their father came in after his long journey across the sky and took the sun from his back, he turned to his woman and said "Who were those two I saw coming this way? Where are they?" "No one came this way," she answered. "Am I blind?" he demanded angrily. "Where are they?" Four times he asked her, getting angrier all the while, until finally the woman said, "Perhaps you should not be talking so much, because the two who came here today were looking for their father. And you told me that you never visit anyone when you go out, that you have met no woman but me. So then—whose children are these?" She pointed to the bundle of robes in which she had hidden the Twins. The Sun Carrier seized the bundle and pulled away the robe of dawn, then the robe of blue sky, then the robe of yellow-evening light, and lastly the robe of darkness, and there the Twins were. He took hold of them at once and threw them at sharp spikes on the east wall, but each Twin held tightly in one hand the life-feather given by the Spider Woman and was not hurt. Again he threw them— to the south, to the west, to the north—and each time they came back to him unharmed.

So then the terrible father tried to cook the Twins to death in a sweatlodge filled with hot steam, but the wind blew in through a crack and cooled them. When they came out their father said, "You must be my children, and so I will give you the pipe to smoke." But that was only a trick because he had filled it with poison. The Twins took the pipe and passed it back and forth, smoking until it was finished, and they even said it tasted sweet.

Then at last their father knew them and was pleased with their courage. "So now my children," he said, "what is it that I can do for you?" They had won his favor and he was proud. And so it was in that good day.

Mrs. M walked back to her desk. "Is that all?" someone asked. "It don't make sense," someone else told her. "They go out lookin for'im an they don't know who he is."

She considered that. "Well, isn't that what we all do? I mean, when you go out to find your love you don't know who it is, right?"

"But why'd they go lookin for'im?" Nestor demanded, his tone tinged with disgust. "They shoulda said to hell with'im!"

"They wanted his help because there were so many monsters then, hunting the people down like animals and eating them."

"Dinosaurs," someone said.

"There wasn't no people when there was dinosaurs," someone said in a doesn't-everybody-know-that tone. "An it was a dumb story. I mean, it was alright but a little dumb, know what I mean?"

"It didn't do nothin for me," someone said.

"Well alright, I tried," Mrs. M told them, "so let's have a little sympathy for the handicapped. But I know that you have some good stories of your own for us today, about people important to you, so let's form our usual groups and we'll hear them."

With a renewal of noise the youngsters, released into sociability, slid their desks and chairs over the floor, forming four groups—three of them arranged in double rows of facing desks, conference table style. Mrs. M sat with a circle of eight—and among them I expected to find the ones in whom she was taking a particular interest.

Amir, perhaps. He read two or three paragraphs telling how his older sister began taking care of him when she was twelve, and after a few questions about this from the others, Mrs. M said "You have a sentence there I think is very beautiful: 'My sister was my childhood.'" She glanced around at the others, gathering confirmation. "You might try making that your first sentence," she added. "I like it the way it is," he said.

Then Gino told us about his father and the way he disciplines a son who gets out of line—which doesn't happen much anymore, Gino assured us. "He's got these big square hands, and he raises his right hand up like he's gonna hit me. I'm watching it, I'm hunching down, and then he spits on me like I'm not worth it." This expression of contempt and the shame it brings, Gino explained, are more effective than a beating would be. "I wipe it off my neck, or maybe it gets on my shoulder, and I feel real bad." The others thought this was very strange, and some insisted that only a few good swats really teach the lesson. They had written about their mothers—women who were the strength of their families, raising their children alone, some of them, and I wondered if Mrs. M should have told that story about searching for a father. And which of these youngsters had attracted her particular interest? As the readings continued she gave the same attention to each, finding something worth commenting on and encouraging the others to do the same.

When we were settled once again for lunch, this time over a steam-table meal of spaghetti and tomato sauce, I said "That story you told about the Twins—it did what you wanted, it settled them down."

"Oh, is that what I wanted?"

"Well, they listened." Why was she making this difficult? "Here you are telling about Navajos in New Mexico but these kids are living in New Jersey—a different world. They're into hanging out around the way and slam dancing and dressing in style—but they listened to you. It's almost like they're children listening to a bedtime story."

"Yes, I think of it that way sometimes. They'll listen to a story that seems to take them away from their everyday surroundings. When Ashton-Warner was teaching Maori children in New Zealand she taught them songs from *H.M.S. Pinafore,* and when she was here in the U.S. she told Maori stories to the American children. All the while warning us not to stifle the native imagery that children bring to school!" She smiled, amused at the irony.

"That image of the father spitting on his son lingers in my mind. But you did have to stifle them some, like when Malcolm was throwing paper wads across the room. And you do it so quietly. Whatever happens you don't get upset, you're always so calm, so easygoing."

"Oh you think so, do you? Well, let me tell you this: my greatest need is to control the urge to kill!" She wasn't smiling. "That's something else Ashton-Warner and I have in common. She was not a sweet old lady."

When we are startled to the point of shock our bodies may seem to go on mechanically as we watch, and now I watched myself pick up a spoon and dip it into a bowl of mixed fruit. "So I recognize the impulse in others," she was saying, "and it makes me feel sympathetic." Then she too reached for a spoon, and we ate together in silence. How could I pick up on this?

"You're interested in the troubled ones," I said finally. "You feel sympathy with their anger, their unhappiness."

"Yes, the ones who are ignored because they're dull or difficult or ugly and make us want to turn away. But we must give our love to the unlovable." She hesitated, looking away into a distance, then smiled as a thought came. "Now Ella—you've noticed her." But I didn't recognize the name. "She sits near the front where she can have a close shot at me."

That one! "You mean that disagreeable, obnoxious girl who sits there finding fault all the time?"

"That's Ella! She feels better when she can spread the misery. So I told her, I said 'Ella, it puzzles me how someone as nice as you are can disagree all the time.' And I gave her a project to work on. She has to tell us a joke and make us laugh."

"Do you think she'll do it?"

"Well, at first she said how could she just get up and start telling a joke? I said 'Come late to class and use it when the secretary calls on you to pay the penalty. You'll start a new trend.' So she's been trying her jokes out on me, and so far they're all putdowns. She's put down the Italians, the Irish, the Poles, the Blacks, the Jews. Her idea of humor is to ridicule someone."

The bell was about to ring, so gathering up our plastic utensils and plates we carried them over to the trash barrel. Then on the way out we passed the table where Riley was finishing his lunch, and Mrs. M turned back to him. "I see you've joined our club," she said. There was a paperclip linked to another dangling from his lapel. "Well, in that case you know the club secret, and so as a member I now ask it of you," and she leaned down so that he could whisper in her ear—a few words and they both laughed. "Keep the faith," she told him, turning to go on, and he said "Oh I will, I will!"

Outside in the corridor I noticed that many youngsters passing on their way to class were displaying a dangling paperclip attached somewhere to their clothing. "The membership in your Clipper Club is growing every day," I said. "You're having a lot of fun with that."

"Oh yes! We have people pleading to be let in. Some of the members want to keep it exclusive but of course there's no way to do that."

"And this started in your fifth period class."

"Yes, we were talking about fads and fashions and style, and I said we could set the fashion for this school, we could have everyone following us. So we started wearing paperclips. But you're not really a member of the club, you understand, unless you know the club secret."

"How can I become a member?"

"Well, you're supposed to prove yourself worthy by doing a task set for you by a member. And then you can be told the secret. But since you've gratified my ego by giving me all this attention the last two weeks, I'll waive the task. Are you prepared to hear the secret?"

"Yes, I think I am." We had reached her classroom and stopped there by the doorway.

"And do you swear to keep our secret, sharing it only with other members of the Clipper Club?"

"I do."

"Then at this time I invest you with the emblem of membership." She reached into a pocket and took out two linked paperclips, which she then attached to my shirt collar. "The secret," she said whispering into my ear as the youngsters passed by, "is this: There is no secret! Keep it to yourself." And she went on into the room to put her books on her desk under the tiger looking down from the wall.

Here was a bleak message, if you took it seriously—and I was sure she did in spite of her casual, easygoing humor. That the life around us is a play of appearances with no underlying significance, no secret waiting to be revealed, except perhaps an individual one concealed within a style designed to use it for some advantage. And it was her style to lead the dance, inventing the steps as she went along—in this case piquing interest with a sign, an ordinary object made exclusive, suggesting a significance known only to a few, gathering in one after another who then discover the emptiness of it all and are released into silent laughter. Humor is irony taken about as far as it will go, and the woman was a humorist.

How many people had she managed to take in with this? Half the school, it seemed, was happily displaying the paperclip badge and trying now to take in the other half with the pretext of conferring an exclusive honor. Or with simply a promise to satisfy the need to belong. I would not have been surprised to see Dr. Fox himself coming along the corridor with a paperclip

or two hanging from his lapel. And Mrs. M was surely happy
to have created this diversion, which was something more than
a diversion—for as a humorist she made it her mission to bring
a sense of the absurd into the routine day and so move us to
transcend it, in spirit if not in fact.

She managed, then, to create her own unique, ironic pleasures.
But somewhere I have heard that a humorist, like a beast of
prey, always walks alone.

Chapter 6

Missing in September

The advantage in walking alone is the freedom one has to follow closely any telltale signs in the movements of others and seize upon whatever food for thought may appear. And the ability to be alone even when others are present and engaging one in lively conversation, perhaps, is a skill every artist must have whose medium is language. For an artist in company is always gathering impressions for later use, and knows that voices may be heard more clearly in retrospect than in the moment. And the work itself, the artful reshaping of miscellaneous personalities and chance events into a coherent and satisfying experience, must be done by the single individual and so requires the practice of loneliness.

To be alone in a schoolroom with twenty or thirty adolescents or more, as Mrs. Martinez was year after year, is to have ample material for creative action. It is remarkable how much some artists have drawn from a narrow range of experience, finding a whole world in a family or a town—and a schoolroom offers the same scope, being an expression of the great social forces which have shaped the institution of which it is a part. A high school—where for years the district superintendent convened all two thousand students in the auditorium each fall to hear him announcing the annual newspaper and magazine subscription contest to raise money for the senior class trip, exhorting them to get out there and sell! And introducing the publisher of a local newspaper who then gave a rousing speech while punctuating his remarks by throwing silver dollars into the clamoring crowd. Afterwards the youngsters would stream noisily out of the auditorium and into classrooms, bringing along their restless hungers and half-formed narratives. And in one of those rooms Mrs. M waited for them alone, ready to practice her art as the single individual, year after year.

But the penalty for being singular is to be misunderstood, and in the beginning she was thought capriciously nonconforming by supervisors and colleagues alike—unpredictable, with some agenda of her own. In short, difficult. Only her generous affability kept her from being let go, because anyone who listens so well must be trying to get the message, she only needs a little more time, they thought. And in time they decided she was not radical but only a bit eccentric, and as that she could be tolerated. Once they had the right name for her they could live with her.

"But people get tired of seeing you around after a while," she said, "even if they like you. The sound of your voice is too familiar. Maybe I should have moved on to another school years ago, when I could have really enjoyed being the new girl in town." Which made me wonder why she had stayed in this one school for so long, until now the time had come for her to retire. Or so she thought, although she could have stayed a few more years. "But when people start saying 'Oh, you're still here?' then it's time to go. I can take a hint."

And she wanted to go without any attention being given. Over the years so many others had come and gone and been forgotten, and now it was her turn and there was nothing noteworthy in that, she thought—no reason to mark her passage with a special gathering, as some who knew her wished. "At a time like this a party is a memorial service," she said, "and I'd rather not attend. Let them find me missing in September." It fell to me as the one who had known her longest to persuade her otherwise.

Perhaps I was not the right person for the job, however, because for one thing I agreed with her. And for another, I could think of no way to bring her around. That would take luck and some very careful maneuvering since she was a woman not easily persuaded, however agreeably she listened. The assistant principal was very concerned about this and he had called me, pleading the case, so in spite of my doubts I agreed to try. She had already rejected the idea so I would have to approach it indirectly, diplomatically. Perhaps a quiet dinner, just the two of us talking over old times, would provide the opportunity. I was looking forward to it, hoping of course that she would be the same as always, for the exemplars of one's youth remain unchanging in memory through the years.

But what I heard from others made me wonder if perhaps the qualities some of us admired in her had finally lost their flexibility and hardened into mannerisms. It was said that she would fix her eyes with a birdlike intensity on the person speaking to her, so expectant that her listening seemed almost coercive and made some people uncomfortable. And her long silences in the classroom had shortened to nervous hesitations, as though perhaps the supreme confidence that had carried everyone with her through the adolescent commotion had finally weakened. She was still quick with the unexpected remark, sometimes too quick, and now it often seemed only amusingly irrelevant or even disconcerting rather than provocative or stimulating. Perhaps her advanced age had removed her so far from others they no longer took her seriously, or had she finally become as she had been named and was now quite eccentric?

So I was prepared for a disappointment when we met early one evening, wondering if perhaps her voice on the phone those past few years had been deceptively reassuring. And all the way to my apartment she was silent, looking out the window of the cab, replying only indifferently to my conversational gambits. She may be tired—and with good reason, I thought. We walked silently through the lobby, and then as we stepped into the elevator she turned to a woman there with white hair and dressed in a nurse's uniform, leaning against the paneling, obviously tired after a long day's work. "Out saving lives again today?" she asked as the door closed.

"Yes!" the woman answered. "And believe me, some of them aren't worth saving. When you get to be eighty or ninety it's time to go. I pray every day I'll get hit by a truck!"

Over the door, numbers appeared and faded sequentially. "Oh yes, a quick exit is best," Mrs. M said, "even if it comes a little too soon," and they nodded in agreement. A stranger there would have thought they'd known each other a long time. My mood brightened considerably. She still enjoyed provoking even strangers, unconcerned about the possibility of giving offense, relying on her empathetic responsiveness to manage the situation. And even giving offense can be the start of an interesting exchange, she would say, so let's take a chance. She was still interested in people. The door slid open and we stepped out, the two women nodding again.

But this talk of making a quick exit was no help to me, given my task of persuading her to take a bow before leaving the stage. As a distraction I began talking about the woman we had seen sitting in the lobby with a huge sheepdog heaped on the floor nearby like a pile of loose wool. She had gone up on the roof when her first dog died and announced to the world that she was going to jump. . . . But this was another exit story, I realized. Yet once started it had to be finished so I went on, telling how the super had reasoned with her there on the roof, saying "After all, Hazel—you can buy another dog." "That's right!" she said, and went down to the pet shop, where she found Heathcliff.

"The first dog was a Russian wolfhound, and it brought her a lot of attention in the street. Life hardly seemed worth living without it." I was opening a bottle of wine. Mrs. M relished a good white.

"Everyone needs attention," she said. "And your friend Hazel must be getting even more of it now with that monster of a dog. She's managed to turn everyone who sees her into an audience."

"Yes, but she only has a life of making entrances. The exit is surely no treat, with the rear end of that dog waddling away. She walks on with Heathcliff and then she walks off—and in between there's no performance. Unless of course you want to hear her tell about washing him. It takes you wouldn't believe how much soap."

"Well, everyone has a theater where the main act goes on every day. You and I are lucky to have a classroom for our performances. With a large captive audience, too."

Now here was a chance for me to get away from all this talk about entrances and exits, rather than babbling on obsessively like this. Our food was heating on the stove, pleasant music was playing in the background, another bottle of wine was ready—surely there was some way to approach the subject indirectly and bring her to a receptive frame of mind. It was important that she do the talking for a while.

"But you don't really perform in a classroom," I said. "You're not always at the front of the room, talking. You say very little—and so then what you do say carries that much more weight. You practice an art of understatement. So I suppose you are performing, but there's a difference. I mean"—was I babbling again?—"a teacher was complaining to me last week that students are so passive, but she wouldn't have that problem if she performed less and listened more, as you do."

"Well, you're overlooking the fact that I have more problems with the youngsters than she does. I'm a big disappointment to some of them. They think I should be doing more of the work, so they go out complaining that I don't teach them anything. And some resent me for poking them out of their hiding places and making them perform. And then of course there are those who figure we aren't doing anything here but talking so they can fool around, and then I have to sit on them. So you see, I have more discipline problems than most teachers, especially in the first few weeks of school. If Dr. Fox hadn't been there to back me up all those years I wouldn't have lasted. So don't recommend me as a model. Which reminds me—do you still go to schools and visit classrooms, looking for answers?"

"Oh yes. And I have a lot of answers now, but no one is asking me the questions." By this time we were at the dinner table, where I had set out a green salad along with linguini and white clam sauce, my specialty. And the wine was making me feel expansive.

"Just last week I spent my mornings in a school in Brooklyn with a teacher there. Someone told me she was doing good work, so I went to see for myself. And she was. She had a roomful of youngsters who were working independently, writing and sharing their work with each other. So on my last day I said, 'The way you work with these youngsters, they must think they're doing all this by themselves. And maybe they're not going to realize until later, when they look back on their days here with you, how important you've been to them.' She said,

'Oh!—I tell them all the time, You'll never have another teacher like me!' ''

Mrs. M nodded thoughtfully, "How sad, that *she* has to say it." That she felt so alone among those children, it seemed to me, having no one to give her specific witness and confirm her to herself. "And she said it to you. I see that you've learned something about listening."

"Yes—thanks to you. And she's probably right, too. Those children may never have another teacher like her. I've certainly never had another like you." The wine was making me sentimental.

"I don't think you'd want another one like me." That was true, of course, and we both smiled at the irony of it.

"You do manage to provoke some people," I said. For it occurred to me that there were in fact others who, for very different reasons, would not want to have another like her around. "What was that controversy a few years back about some classroom newspaper you started?"

"Oh, it was only a one-page affair—but we printed an article about the student court. We wondered why the defendants were mostly from the housing project and the court officials were from the other side of town. And that agitated the social studies department because this court was their project, their practical lesson in self-government, in democracy. They said we had no business criticizing it. By the way, we called our newspaper *The People's Voice*. We had a bigger circulation than the school newspaper for a few issues, but then our paper supply was cut off. Economy, of course. But we had a good time while it lasted."

"And the student court—how long did that last?"

"Only until the end of the year. I like to think we helped kill it."

No wonder there would be sighs of relief from some as she departed—and they wanted to mark the occasion in some way. But now I was passing from sentimentality to cynicism, and none of this was helping me to achieve the goal.

"You know that Marvin wants to have a dinner for you," I said. "And he thinks maybe you could tell us how the school has changed in the years you've been there. But you know, I think we could contrive a more fitting exit—something a little more creative. One last jolt."

"A parting shot, you mean? Oh no, that's not my way. I want to go quietly, with no fuss at all."

"But this isn't like you, thinking only of yourself. Some of us don't want you to simply disappear. We're at a turning point in our lives. I mean, you won't be there when we look for you now, we'll have to look *back*, which means that suddenly we're much older than we thought we were. Your leaving is a stage on life's way for some of us, and we want to mark the occasion. We want to feel sorry for ourselves."

"You've touched my heart," she said. "So let's have the dinner, and I'll get up and tell them I've changed my mind, I'm going to stay another five years." She laughed, and so did I at the thought of how faces would look on hearing that.

"Now let's be serious. Think of Marvin. I mean, he was one of your students too—and so your leaving means that he's not a student any more. There'll be no one there calling him Marvin, he can really be Mister Assistant Principal at last. That dinner means a lot to him. In fact, a number of people are going to feel a certain relief with your leaving, so let's give them a chance to show their appreciation and they'll finally be done with you. You see the irony of it, don't you?"

"Well, I hadn't thought of looking at it that way. You have a point. And I admire the devious mind that could think of it." She took a sip of coffee and sat there contemplatively for a moment. "Alright. We'll have a nice dinner with a few of our friends. And I want this to be in a place with music, like that Italian restaurant you took me to years ago. Do you remember?" I did, and the restaurant was still there.

Marvin was delighted. He reserved a dining room and invited twenty or more people—many more than Mrs. M had specified. "But there's to be no ceremony," I told him. "Just a few friends having dinner together." Yes, yes, he nodded. "I think we should have flowers," he said. "And the piano, and maybe a violin too." I called Mrs. M to say that perhaps she might prepare a few remarks for the occasion. "Oh, let's keep this very informal," she said. "No one wants to hear speeches at dinner. I'll improvise." So one Saturday evening at the end of June we came up Eighth Avenue together in a taxi to Rienzi's Italian Garden.

On the way, as we sat talking quietly, I felt something under my hand and found a wallet on the seat. Empty, of course. Mrs. M held it up for the driver to see, saying "Someone left you a nice wallet back here."

"Yeah," he said, "there's nothin in it. Like every day in this cab." He was putting the pressure on us for a good tip already.

"So you look back here after the passengers get out," Mrs. M said. "You must find some good things left behind now and then."

"Yeah, now an then. Had a good one last week. This lady gets outa the cab, see, an she drops some bills right by the curb and walks away."

"I'll bet you called after her real loud."

"Yeah, I rapped on the winda wid a sponge." We laughed with him, enjoying his pleasure in his good fortune. No small town virtues here in the big city, I thought. You take care of Number One first. We like to think that in a classroom we escape for a time this calculus of gain, but of course that can't be true. The driver braked suddenly, swerved around a car ahead and we raced on.

After a moment Mrs. M turned back to me. "You know, last night I was looking through the old yearbooks, wondering what's happened to all those youngsters. There've been so many of them. All that energy and talent, and you wonder if anything ever came of it out there in the world. Do you remember Dan, who used to write those songs? He gave up music for cocaine. And your friend Jerry went to jail. And one face looked so familiar, but not the name. Ella Cottam. And then I remembered. She changed her name and went to California, and I'd see her on television now and then. She didn't seem to have any ability at all in high school. There's no way of predicting what some people will do. She killed herself. And she left a note. 'Why not walk with me once in the moonlight and call me love?'" This was not the mood appropriate to the occasion, I thought, but no distraction occurred to me. "She was in such a hurry," Mrs. M said.

When we arrived at Rienzi's the others were already there,

waiting for us at the bar in cheerful conviviality. This was the small intimate group I'd hoped for—only eleven people and not the twenty or more Marvin had invited. These few, I thought. Mrs. M took a glass of wine and moved along greeting one after another, meeting wives and husbands, until Marvin led her into the dining room, the rest of us following noisily. As we came in the pianist struck up "Oh Marie" on the spinet by the door. I noticed that Marvin had forgone the lavish floral display, leaving the dusty plastic flowers on their corner stands. In fact, the room retained its usual Neopolitan charm, with checkered-cloth-covered tables standing on the dark uneven wood floor, and one wall softly lighted to display a mural of Naples with Vesuvius smoking in the background and a tenor in the foreground serenading his love looking down from a balcony. Marvin guided Mrs. M to a few tables that had been pulled together under the mural, and she sat down not far from Vesuvius while the rest of us found places as chance or ongoing conversation suggested.

Riley and his wife joined me at one end of this makeshift banquet table, along with a young man who turned out to be a commodities broker from Chicago. Two waitresses dressed in what seemed to be their own version of peasant dress, with bandanna and dangling earrings, colorful blouse and petticoated skirt, came in carrying bottles of wine and began filling our glasses. At one end of the room a buffet table stood crowded with covered pans and heavy china. This was just the tacky atmosphere that promised a really good party.

As we settled back down at the table with our plates of food, Riley went on telling the young man—Matt—the story of the Clipper Club. "The strange thing about it," he said, "was that when I went into my classroom wearing the paperclips, all the kids who had them were on my side, they worked with me. Of course by the end of the week everyone was wearing them and the effect was gone. It would make a study for a sociologist. I don't know how she could think of those things."

"I missed that," Matt said, "but I'll tell you something else she did. See, I wouldn't write anything. A couple of sentences an that was it. I wouldn't write anything else unless I knew it was gonna be good, an so I didn't write anything. An I had this pen I liked that wrote with a very fine line. She called it my wimpy pen. So she gave me a pen with this thick point but I wouldn't use it, it was like a little kid writing. I wanted everything to look perfect, it had to be just right. So one day they're all sittin there writing, and I'm just sittin there, an she takes me outa the room. She says 'Look up there.' She's lookin up over the door. She says 'You see that sign I put up there every day?' I'm lookin but there's nothin there. She says 'It's right there in letters three inches high. Anything goes! So come on, feel free, loosen up!' She tells me to look up there every day an I'll see it. An she says 'Keep it to yourself.' So every day I'm lookin up there, an I swear after a while I could see it."

Riley and I looked at each other and nodded. "Just like her," he said. I turned back to Matt. "Tell me something. How did you ever get to be a commodities broker?"

"Oh, I knocked around for a few years after high school, I didn't know what to do. I went to California, I went to Chicago. An I'm staying with this friend of mine in Chicago, so one day he takes me to work with him. He was a runner on the floor of the commodities exchange. An the minute I walked onto the floor an saw the action an heard the noise I knew this was the place. Here's where I'm gonna make it! I could see myself in the middle of it with those guys betting on the market. So I got a job as a runner an I learned the business. You know how in Las Vegas the odds are in favor of the house? Well, I'm the house." He looked away for a moment. "In high school," he said, "I was the kid with bad teeth."

"But how did you know about this party?" Riley asked.

"Oh, that's another story. It's June an my kids are gettin out of school, so I was thinking about Mizzem an I called information an got her number. I said 'You'll never guess who this is,' an she said 'Yes I will, it's Matt Coleman.' I couldn't believe it! I said 'How do you know?' an she said 'Because I've been thinking about you.' An she asked me to come. Isn't that strange?"

The peasant girls were once more pouring wine and the piano player was well into "Amore," joined by a few festive voices from the other end of the table. I was hoping the informality would continue since Mrs. M wanted no speeches, but Marvin was shifting in his chair, looking as though he were waiting to seize the moment, half rising then settling back. Finally he took a spoon and rapped on his glass for attention, provoking an answering chorus of glassy tones from around the table while he looked right and left, grinning happily and waiting. The wine had made him somewhat more than cheerful and, as we soon found, sentimental as well.

"You all know why we're here," he said, turning in his chair to nod at Mrs. M. "We're here because—well, you know why we're here. So I just want to say a few things about this friend of ours here." And he went on to speak of the many lives that Mrs. M had touched, of how so many felt so much for her, of the dedication to her work that kept her in that school through the years, and so on. This was just the sort of talk she had hoped to avoid, and as Marvin went on with wine-wobbly enthusiasm she stared down at her plate, withdrawing as a participant to become a spectator. "And now," Marvin said, "perhaps our dear friend has a few last words for us. No, no, that's not what I mean. You know what I mean . . ."

"Now just a moment!" Mrs. M said. She was not smiling. "You need to know one thing right now. It wasn't dedication that kept me in that school all those years. Oh no! It was curiosity. I wanted to be around long enough to see how you all turned out." She looked around at us, nodding. "And much to my surprise you've all done very well." Of course we laughed appreciatively, pleased with ourselves, but I remembered that on the way here she had been talking about some who had not turned out so well.

"And there was no reason for me to go anywhere else when so much was happening in our school. It's changed so much over the years, I feel as if I've taught in three or four different schools. When I first came we were all middle-class and white, and there was no need to question what we were doing. Then the minority students began to come, and the housing project was built, and then we had to explain what we were doing and that wasn't easy. They woke us up. Of course we had some rough times but that was the real world we were living in, and Dr. Fox was there to see us through. I can still see him standing every morning way down at the end of the main corridor, punctuating it like an exclamation mark. Marvin told me a story

about him just now, and I think he'd like to share it with you."
She turned to him.

"Yeah, well—I guess you don't know about this unless you
got into trouble all the time. Get into enough trouble and they'd
send you in to see Dr. Fox. And he'd be looking at you across
the desk, and you'd be sitting there nervous, hangin tough, and
then he'd say 'Are you learning your skills?' It was like the
other stuff wasn't worth talking about. He'd ask you about math
and social studies and English, and then he'd tell you to come
back next week and tell him what you'd learned. And then
when you're going out he'd say 'Don't get sent in here again,'
and you knew if you did he'd make you disappear."

A big man at the other end of the table nodded vigorously.
"Do you remember when the guys on the football team let their
hair grow," he said, "and the coaches didn't like it, they were
trying to make us get haircuts? And Dr. Fox said 'What we want
on the team are gorillas so let'em look like gorillas.' He was
quite a guy."

"I had this argument with him once," one of the women said,
"about—well alright, it was about flying saucers. Now don't
laugh at me. You remember how he used to teach a class
sometimes, be a substitute?—and we got to arguing about flying
saucers. And he said, 'You'll live out your whole life and never
see one, and in your old age you'll remember I told you this.'
I've never forgotten that. I *can't* forget it."

"So you're still looking for one," someone said and we laughed.

By now the room was becoming noisy as the overflow
customers from the main dining room were seated nearby and
the piano player, who had been taking a break, returned to his
instrument with renewed enthusiasm. The flow of reminiscence
gradually receded until we were sitting there nearly silent,
knowing the party was over and the time had come for us to
part, but no one was quite ready to make the move. Then as
Marvin was about to stand, Mrs. M rested a hand on his arm
and he settled back.

"My friends," she said, and we could just hear her over the
surrounding noise of conversation and piano, "this evening we
have enjoyed good company, good conversation, and good wine.
So now I would like to say one more thing. And this should be

spoken to each of you, one person to another, so I will say it to Marvin here, and he will pass it on to the next, and so on until we have all heard and said the words." What last turn would she give our evening now, I wondered?

Leaning toward Marvin she said something to him quietly, and then he turned to his wife and spoke to her. So the words were passed around the table, one to another, until Riley's wife turned to me and said, "Go in beauty."

Author

John Rouse has taught in the public schools of New York and New Jersey and was the first director of the Oceanics program, a school for troubled youngsters aboard a square-rigger in the Atlantic Ocean. He is now with the English department of St. Peter's College in Jersey City. His previously published work includes *The Completed Gesture: Myth, Character, and Education.*

TF   IF